F

USE THE
POWER
OF
YOUR
DREAMS TO
TRANSFORM
YOUR LIFE

# Night
AND
# Day

*Jack*
*Maguire*

A Roundtable Press Book

A Fireside Book
Published by Simon & Schuster Inc.
New York   London   Toronto   Sydney   Tokyo

**FIRESIDE**

SIMON AND SCHUSTER BUILDING
ROCKEFELLER CENTER
1230 AVENUE OF THE AMERICAS
NEW YORK, NEW YORK 10020

A ROUNDTABLE PRESS BOOK

FIRESIDE AND COLOPHON ARE REGISTERED TRADEMARKS
OF SIMON & SCHUSTER INC.

DESIGNED BY DIANE STEVENSON / SNAP·HAUS GRAPHICS

MANUFACTURED IN THE UNITED STATES OF AMERICA

1 2 3 4 5 6 7 8 9 10

LIBRARY OF CONGRESS CATALOGING IN PUBLICATION DATA

MAGUIRE, JACK.
NIGHT AND DAY / JACK MAGUIRE.
P. CM.
"A FIRESIDE BOOK."
"A ROUNDTABLE PRESS BOOK."
1. DREAMS.   2. SELF-REALIZATION.   3. DREAMS—PROBLEMS,
EXERCISES,   ETC.   4. SELF-REALIZATION—PROBLEMS, EXERCISES, ETC.
FD10 3-6-89.   I. TITLE.
BF1091.M337   1989      154.6′3—DC20
89-31505
CIP

ISBN 0-671-65845-X

FOR PERMISSION TO REPRINT FROM THE FOLLOWING WORK,
THE AUTHOR GRATEFULLY ACKNOWLEDGES:
*GULLIVER'S TRAVELS,* BY JONATHAN SWIFT.
NEW YORK: CROWN PUBLISHERS, INC., 1985.
*THE VARIETY OF DREAM EXPERIENCE,* BY DR. MONTAGUE ULLMAN AND
CLAIRE LIMMER NEW YORK: CONTINUUM, 1987.
*WORKING WITH DREAMS,* BY DR. MONTAGUE ULLMAN AND NAN ZIMMERMAN.
NEW YORK: JEREMY P. TARCHER, INC., 1982.

To MY SISTER,
KELLI MAUREEN MAGUIRE

# $\mathcal{A}$cknowledgments

I'm very grateful to Marsha Melnick, Susan Meyer, and Meg Ross of Roundtable Press for their invaluable support and guidance in helping me put this book together. I'm also indebted to Barbara Gess of Simon & Schuster, whose faith in this book's message made its publication possible.

# Contents

# 1

# Dreams and Dreamwork

OCCASIONALLY WHEN YOU are outdoors on a clear, sunny day, you may see the moon—a pale, matte version of its luminous, nighttime self, but still a haunting presence in the sky. Whenever I see it, I think of how my father once compared this mildly disorienting phenomenon to the lingering effect of dreams. Every so often, he asked me, don't you have a dream that stays with you during the day, puzzling you or making you feel happy or sad? Indeed, I did and still do have such dreams.

Although my father's analogy failed to explain why I could see the moon during the day (my original question), it nevertheless triggered a revelation. I suddenly understood that dreams constitute a second life. Like the moon reflecting the sun, our dreams reflect our daylight life, but they also have an independent existence. They are powerful in their own right, just as the moon is with its gravitational force; and they can exert that power during our waking hours as well as our sleeping hours.

In the years that followed, I clung to this basic concept of what dreams are and what they can do; and it helped me keep my bearings as I explored the immense body of scholarly dream literature that has accumulated down through the ages. Quirky or exhilarating as it can sometimes be, it's depressing reading in the long run. On the one hand, most of these works focus obsessively on the *causes* of dreams at the expense of talking about the *effects* of dreams; and since the causes of dreams, like the causes of life itself, continue to defy definition, even the most accomplished writers on the subject leave the general reader feeling confused and unsatisfied. On the other hand, prevailing theories about the nature of dreams have grown progressively less inspirational as time and technology have marched along.

At the beginning of recorded history, and for millennia thereafter, dreams were considered divine messages in virtually every religious culture. The Sphinx of Gizeh bears a chest plaque honoring a dream of the future pharaoh Thotmosis IV, who slept between the Sphinx's outstretched paws and heard him command the repair of his monument. In the biblical tradition, Yahweh frequently uses dreams to communicate with his chosen people, as Job affirms: "God speaks to man in one way, and in two, though man does not perceive it. In a dream, in a vision of the night, when deep sleep falls upon men, while they slumber in their beds, then He opens the ears of men" (Job 33.12). Joseph of the New Testament learns through a dream that Mary will be the mother of Jesus; while Maya, the mother of Buddha, actually conceives her holy son in a dream. Mohammed's mission comes to him in a series of dream-visits from the Archangel Gabriel; and a dream of Mohammed's companion, Abdullah ben Zayd, serves as the inspiration for the *ad-han* itself, the daily call to prayer, as well as for the words to be spoken by the *muezzin,* or caller: "There is no god but God, and Mohammed is His prophet."

As societies assumed an increasingly secular character and sacred dogma replaced revelation, dreams were officially devalued. The intelligentsia weren't sure what to make of dreams anymore, so they became objects of folk wisdom by default. At best, individual poets and healers might champion the oracular ability of dreams to reflect a dreamer's identity and fate; at worst, dreams were accused of being hallucinations or demonic possessions. In balance, however, people continued to believe that dreams were essentially super-natural mysteries, even through the Age of Reason on up to the end of the last century.

Everything changed with the publication of Sigmund Freud's *Interpretation of Dreams* in 1900. Using his own dreams as guides, Freud developed a compelling theory that a person's dreams portray his or her unique set of repressed (usually infantile) sexual urges, most often in a disguised form, since the material is too shocking to be confronted directly. With this kind of dream-study as its cornerstone, psychoanalysis, a therapeutic discipline that is part science and part art, swiftly became the brave new authority on the human mind and soul. Once again, people took their dreams seriously, but only as symptoms of abnormality.

Roughly twenty years later, Carl Gustav Jung, one of Freud's disciples, broke with Freud and established a more broad-based and positive theory about dreams. In Jungian terms, dreams are spontaneous and direct creative acts drawing upon symbolic images that are common to all human beings and lie at the very core of the human psyche (a core that Jung called "the collective uncon-scious"). Dreams were suddenly not just dirty sex anymore, but somehow they remained close to the soil—the stuff of anthropo-logical and archaeological digs rather than ladders to heaven.

Now, organized science is bold enough to consider the possibility that dreams are nothing but neurological garbage. Perhaps I should say "junk" instead of "garbage," since the operative metaphor is high technology. Psychiatrists Robert McCarley and J. Allan Hob-son of the Harvard Medical School claim there is a "dream state generator" located in the brain stem that fires neurons randomly to higher brain centers controlling such functions as vision, hearing, balance, movement, and emotion. Forced to make sense of these weak, incoherent signals, the brain weaves the best story it can—sort of a fractured fairy tale. "They [dreams] are ambiguous stimuli," states Hobson, "which can be interpreted in any way a thera-pist is predisposed to."

Taking the McCarley-Hobson theory even further, Dr. Francis Crick of the Salk Institute in La Jolla, California, and his associate Dr. Graeme Mitchison of Cambridge University in England propose that the function of dreams is to "unlearn" false or nonproductive connections that the brain has accumulated during the day, so that it can continue running smoothly. Thus a dream, in computer lan-guage, is a form of "off-line" processing; and the effort to re-member dream images may even be harmful. "We dream in order to forget," Crick and Mitchison write.

*Night and Day* focuses on the actual *effects* of dreams in the lives of dreamers, rather than on the possible *causes* of the dreaming process in the human brain. Any of the above theories about causes may be true. I even suspect that all of them are true, with individual dreams having a combination of causes and different kinds of dreams having different combinations of causes. But that's another issue.

What bothers me about these cause-related approaches to dreams (particularly in the twentieth century) is that they are full of hidden assumptions that subtly discourage the average dreamer from working with his or her dreams.* The three most damaging assumptions are: first, that the cause of a phenomenon dictates its meaning; second, that one can't, or shouldn't, pay attention to a phenomenon that lacks clear meaning, even though it impresses itself continually and dramatically on one's life; and third, that if a dream has countless potential interpretations, some contradictory to others, it has no "real" meaning.

The main purpose of *Night and Day* is to demonstrate that dreams acquire value in the world of the dreamer according to how he or she uses them. Like any episode in waking life, a dream may

*In popular culture, and, therefore, in this book, the word "dreamwork" and the expression "working with a dream" refer to the conscious, often methodical, effort one puts into understanding a dream. These usages are not to be confused with Freud's definition of "dreamwork" as the actual production of a dream within the human mind.

possess one magical message or it may contain multitudes of possible messages: some magical, some not. What's important to remember is that a dream winds up meaning what one makes of it, and that a dream can mean a great deal.

As I've just illustrated, a certain amount of theorizing is inevitable in any book on dreams. The ideas in this book, however, will be derived from what I've learned through my own night and day experiences as well as through the night and day experiences that others have shared with me.

Here is what I believe dreams can do for all of us, and what *Night and Day* can do for you:

---

■ **Dreams can connect us with feelings that might otherwise go unexpressed or unrecognized.**

---

When we recall a dream, the dominant element in our memory is likely to be the emotions it aroused. Many times, these emotions are pleasurable—tinged with the freedom of time and circumstances that is unique to dream life. More often, however, these emotions are so naked, overpowering, indefinable, or unfamiliar that our rational mind rejects them, just as it does in waking life. For this reason, we're inclined to forget a large number of our dreams or lump them all together as "disturbing."

The emotional play and education that dream life offers, however, can add much to the quality of our existence. From day to day, our waking life, dominated by conscious concerns, confines itself to a severely limited range of emotions; but from night to night, our dream life can compensate. It can remind us how it feels to be triumphant, vanquished, beloved, loving, gregarious, solitary, childlike, mature, true, false, and so on, in order that we may stay emotionally prepared to live richer and more productive lives, no matter what happens.

Dreams also provide us with revealing pictures of our short-term and long-term inner climate—how we truly feel, which can be too ineffable, complicated, unpleasant, or irrational for the conscious mind to articulate without some inspirational prompting. If, for example, you're forced in a dream to play barefoot basketball with team members who delight in throwing tacks under your feet, you may be alerted to a serious problem you're having with colleagues at work that you've never faced in your waking life because you couldn't put it into images, much less words. In this respect, dreams are a sixth sense: a source of intuition as well as a medium of communication.

*Night and Day* offers you self-assessment frameworks for exploring both your waking-life feelings and your dream-life feelings, so that you can draw meaningful connections between them. As it reviews individual case histories, it also helps you learn by example. Using these case histories as models, you can develop your own methods for achieving greater emotional flexibility and for translating your feelings into constructive actions.

■ **Dreams speak for themselves—they are stimulating and illuminating experiences in their own right.**

To put it simply, dreams are adventures we have when we are sleeping. And now scientists are beginning to confirm what humanists have always believed: Dreams can make the same kinds of contributions to our memories, thoughts, feelings, and behaviors as our waking experiences can. The critical difference is that dreams take us to worlds that are distinctly out of the ordinary, where we can gather all sorts of novel impressions unavailable to us in our everyday frames of reference. As Dr. Thomas Cowan, founder of the Brooklyn Dream Community, says:

*Dreams are doorways into other realities. Whether or not we understand the meaning of our dreams the next morning doesn't really matter. They have still taken us there. Alice could never figure out the rules for*

*Wonderland, but that was not the point. The point about being in Wonderland is being there. The most important truth about the Land of Oz is that it isn't Kansas anymore.*

Deriving benefit from a dream, in fact, is very much like deriving benefit from a work of art. Certainly the more critical intelligence you bring to bear on a novel, painting, or poem, the more insights you can gain and the stronger the impact of the work can be on your life. Still, the main event is to experience the work of art all by itself. You don't have to know, for example, who Mona Lisa was in the life of Leonardo da Vinci, how he came to paint her, or the compositional logic that accounts for her pose in order to admire her portrait and be intrigued by her smile.

*Night and Day* gives you both a scientific and a grassroots perspective on why what dreams *do* is just as important as what dreams *mean*. It prepares you to have fun in and with your dream life by recalling dreams more vividly, appreciating different styles of dreaming, managing nightmares, inducing dreams on topics that you select, becoming more conscious (or "lucid") during dreams, and even orchestrating dreams as they unfold. It will also give you blueprints for assisting others to have a more enjoyable dream life and for sharing dreams safely and pleasurably in a social context.

---

## ■ Dreams can assist us to develop and achieve personal goals.

---

We are entering what Carl Sagan calls "The Age of the Mind." Increasingly sophisticated technology is uncovering and spreading new evidence about how the mind functions and how we can affect the mind's performance, and much of this evidence points to the value of working with our dreams. In personal, social, academic, and business life, a higher premium is being placed on creativity and problem-solving skills, leading many people to tap their "dream genius" for inspiration and insight. And while psychiatrists and psychologists have been relying on dream analysis for decades as a therapeutic aid, now laypeople are choosing to follow their dreams independently in order to achieve greater self-awareness, interact more effectively with others, and enhance the way they respond to life's challenges.

The annals of dream literature abound with stories of great dreams that enabled their dreamers to accomplish amazing things. Albert Einstein, for example, attributed the origin of his famous theory of relativity to a dream he had when he was a teenager. During the dream, he was sliding downhill on a sled at night, and the sled picked up so much speed that the stars began to assume wondrously different patterns and colors. His entire scientific career, he later claimed, could be viewed as a meditation on that one dream; and he remarked on several occasions during his lifetime that access to one's dreams is the key to original thought.

When it comes to dreams, the stuff of legends is also the stuff of everynight and everyday experiences. *Night and Day* is written to help you make the most of those experiences. It details how individual dreamers achieved practical results by interpreting their dreams according to their own interests, ambitions, and lifestyles and by finding their own ways to act on their interpretations.

Specifically, *Night and Day* examines different personal life objectives relating to self-fulfillment, human relationships, problem solving, and creativity and assists you to set your own goals in each of these areas (with or without input from your dreams). Then it discusses how working with dreams can help you attain the goals you've set.

---

■ **The more we cultivate our dream life, the richer and more rewarding it becomes.**

---

Dreams live up to what we expect of them. If we belittle their significance, make no effort to remember them, or never do anything with them, then they won't amount to much except by accident. This is true of waking-life situations as well, with one major difference. In the case of our waking life, other factors can and do influence us to apply what we experience toward fulfilling ourselves, nurturing our relationships, solving our problems, and exercising our creativity. In the case of our dream life, that responsibility rests totally on us.

It's understandable that we're inclined to put off responsibilities for which the outside world does not hold us to account. But we ignore our dreams at our peril. Dreams are not sporadic, fortuitous events but systematic features of our sleeping lives, night after night. We may dismiss them, but they don't go away; and whether we accept it or not, they have a role in forming our personalities and life histories.

In 1953, clinical studies at the University of Chicago conducted by Professor Nathaniel Kleitman and his student Eugene Aserinsky established that human beings—and most other animals, for that matter—exhibit rapid eye movement (known as REM) during dreams. In other words, we use the same physical eye activity to follow our dream visions that we use to follow the sights of our waking life. By clocking the REM sleep of numerous volunteers who spent the night at their laboratory, Kleitman and Aserinsky demonstrated for the first time in history that all human beings dream during each night's sleep. In fact, their studies proved that a human being typically dreams four or five times a night, in roughly ninety-minute cycles. Previously, it had been assumed that different people had radically different dreaming histories—an understandable misconception because different people exhibit widely different degrees of dream recall.

Since we do lead an extensive dream life in any event and since our dream life is intricately involved with our waking life, we're not only wasting a valuable resource for living by not getting actively involved in our dreams, we're also allowing ourselves to become victims of our dreams—passively yielding to repetitive, potentially destructive dream-life patterns when we could easily "wise up" and do better.

Above all, the aim of *Night and Day* is to keep you alert to your dreams and to stimulate you to think about them in new ways, so that you can avoid the trap of living only a half life through forgetfulness or negligence. Toward this end, the text offers numerous step-by-step experiments you can perform with dreams and the material they yield; but it's sufficient simply to borrow suggestions from these experiments for your own customized work with dreams, mindful that you can conduct these experiments step by step when and if you so desire.

*Night and Day* is not a book that tells you that you need to change or improve yourself. It helps you realize that you owe it to yourself to give your dreams some loving care.

The path that led me to write *Night and Day* is full of loops and curves, which is appropriate considering the subject matter. It's a path worth describing, not only to establish the background that informs this book, but also to clarify some of its major themes. The path begins and ends with the keeping of a dream journal, a practice I've followed fairly consistently since the time I was twelve years old—not too long after I started wondering why I could sometimes see the moon during the day.

My dream journal fed my interest in the humanities throughout high school and college; and ultimately, during graduate school, it led me to choose "The Influence of Dreams on the Twentieth-Century Novel" as the subject for my doctoral dissertation. At this point, I'd been regularly exchanging dreams and dream talk with literature majors for almost a decade, so it seemed like a paper I could, figuratively speaking, compose in my sleep.

In rough draft, the dissertation began with James Joyce and concluded with Jack Kerouac. The issue of whether Joyce deliberately tried to invent the language of the dreaming mind in his 1939 epic *Finnegan's Wake* (thereby adding symbolic freight to the title word "wake") is hotly debated in literary circles; but at least it's a theory based directly on the words of the author, who wrote in a 1926 letter discussing the work in progress: "One great part of every human existence is passed in a state which cannot be rendered sensible by the use of wideawake language, cutanddry grammar and goahead plot."

I like to believe the *Finnegan's Wake* "dream language" theory; and I still find it enormously helpful to think of my dreaming mind as speaking a foreign language: one that is difficult for my waking mind to master, but well worth a try, since it's a language that is native to a major part of me. This perspective gives me the patience to write my dreams down as *they* speak, rather than in the polished and facile language of reason, and to spend more energy on translating what my dreams are really saying, instead of imposing a "quick-fix" explanation on them or throwing them in the jibberish bin.

As for Kerouac, the existence of a strong link between his dreams and his novels is irrefutable. His 1961 publication, *Book of Dreams,* which contains excerpts from almost twenty years' worth of his personal dream journals, actually keys his dream characters to characters in his novels. It also provides a fascinating evolutionary drama of how certain images came to dominate his dreaming and waking lives and serve as catalysts for his art—haunting images that are common and yet magical, such as the cool-hot sheen of red neon light on an old brick wall, sharp stars that blossom softly through tears in upturned eyes, the body of a continent rolling beneath one's feet.

Through Kerouac, then, I learned two more important lessons about dreams. First, they keep our minds fresh and creative, ever able to make the ordinary seem mysterious and the mysterious seem ordinary. Second, they preserve our most treasured images, our personal life-symbols, recasting them again and again to give our life as a whole its special character.

Joyce and Kerouac inspired me in other ways as well. I was so fired up with an idea for a novel that I decided to work on it right away rather than finish my dissertation. While I did this, I worked nights as an emergency blood bank technician at Boston University Hospital and inadvertently entered my most intense period of dreaming to date.

My job required me to sleep overnight at the hospital and be available, on call, whenever blood needed to be typed, cross-matched, or transfused. Every one or two hours during the night I'd be awakened by a call; and almost always, I'd be interrupted in the middle of a dream. Many of my dreams at this time involved characters, moods, situations, or locales in my novel; and I found that I could continue such dreams, simply by wanting to, when I returned to sleep. Soon I began manipulating my dreams, incubating certain scenarios and testing them; and weeks later, I discovered I could even stage-manage dreams as I went along (a phenomenon known as "lucid dreaming," or becoming conscious that you are dreaming *while* you are dreaming).

Just as my doctorate fell victim to my dreams, so did my novel. The plot got further and further out of hand as my dreaming mind gave it all sorts of fantastic embellishments. I came to realize that I was more enamored of having fun with creating fiction than with completing a novel. As a result, I no longer pressured myself to produce a publishable manuscript. The decision was liberating and gave me a sense of what was truly important to me. Despite all the apparently false trails I pursued during this stage of my waking life, it was, in balance, a very happy and productive time. It brought me fascinating, firsthand dream adventures, and it steered me in a direction I've never regretted following: becoming a teacher, a writer, and a dream-advocate.

For a number of years after graduate school, I taught composition and literature classes at Memphis State University. Often I assigned creative writing projects involving dreams; always I encouraged students to keep dream journals and review them for essay ideas. Through my students' work, I learned that keeping a dream journal on a regular basis can help virtually anyone become more comfortable and proficient in his or her writing skills. After all, dream journal writers do not have to be inhibited about following a particular structure or syntax, nor do they have to worry about finding subject matter (assuming they can remember their dreams from time to time). My students also demonstrated to me that examining one's dreams is an excellent way to deepen one's understanding of how symbolic expression works. The more we observe how our own dreaming mind infuses certain images with special meaning and then weaves patterns among these images, the more insight we have into the creative efforts of other individuals.

In time, I moved to New York City and launched a career as a writer and communications consultant. Here my interest in dreams came into much sharper focus. Through seminars led by Dr. Montague Ullman, founder of the Dream Laboratory at Maimonides Medical Center, I learned the mechanics and value of experiential dreamwork—that is, dream analysis informed by the dreamer's own judgments, emotions, and instincts rather than some exterior theory about dreams. Using Ullman's methodology as well as others, I started participating in small weekly dream groups, where I was not only challenged to dig deeper into my dreams than I had on my own, but also exposed to the amazingly various ways in which different people dream and process their dreams.

In addition to Ullman, I met many other multitalented, courageous, and exciting dream activists who had organized their own dreamwork enterprises. Among these early contacts were John Perkins, leader of the New York Dream Community, a workshop center and "clearinghouse" for the growing number of individuals and groups practicing dreamwork in metropolitan New York City; Barbara Shor, founder of Dreamgates, one of the more inventive Manhattan dream groups, experimenting with everything from simple dream discussion to dream divination, re-entry, and telepathy; and Bill Stimson, creator of the *Dream Network Bulletin,* an internationally distributed newsletter in which both professional and amateur dreamworkers share experiences and advertise for dream groups and projects.

As time went by, I became more and more involved in amateur dreamwork. In 1983, I helped Tom Cowan found and manage the

Brooklyn Dream Community, which was modeled on Perkins's New York Dream Community and offered monthly workshops on dream-related activities for three years. Through this organization, I met Chris Hudson, who succeeded Bill Stimson as publisher of the *Dream Network Bulletin*. For two years (1983–1985), I was an editor of the *Dream Network Bulletin* under Hudson's dynamic leadership; and it was this position that enabled me to see into the heart of what is now commonly known as "the dreamwork movement."

A hybrid product of the self-help, alternative health therapy, consciousness-raising, and human potential movements of the 1960s and 1970s, the dreamwork movement is largely a grassroots affair. The grassroots image notwithstanding, the movement is especially vigorous in large urban areas, where the heavy impact of uncaring crowds and technology exerts more pressure on the individual to look inward for personal meaning and guidance. Of course, committed dreamworkers can also be found in rural settings, where the contrast between nature and civilization can be examined more clearly. According to Dick McLeester, who designs and conducts dream workshops in the New England area, "People in today's society are searching for ways that they can integrate their inner lives with the world around them. There's a lot of change going on and people are seeking a way to make sense of that."

By common agreement, the father of the modern dreamwork movement is Henry Reed, now a licensed professional counselor in Virginia Beach, Virginia. Reed first became interested in dreams during the late 1960s, while he was working toward his doctorate at UCLA and studying dream psychology. At that time, he was also wrestling with alcoholism. When all of his other sobriety campaigns failed, he had a series of graphic dreams that did the trick—notably one revolting nightmare that associated wine with pus oozing from open sores.

So impressed was Reed by the curative power of his dreams that he formed a new life ambition: to free dreamwork from the separate ghettos of psychiatric therapy and occult practice and to return it to the dreamers themselves. Asked to describe his role as one of the early architects of popular dreamwork, he modestly claims, "All I did really was bring up-to-date a tradition that is long-standing, especially among American Indians."

In keeping with his neoshamanic philosophy, Reed derived his idea for fostering lay-led dream groups from a dream—one that had a spellbinding way of linking dreamwork experiences old and new, amateur and professional. As the dream began, Reed and some of his psychologist colleagues were stumbling around in the dark. Eventually, they started moving their bodies in rhythmic, almost ceremonial ways, and the dreamscape burst into light and color. He memorialized this dream in the title of a newsletter he published during the late 1970s, the *Sundance Community Dream Journal,* which functioned as a pioneer medium for inspiring dreamers across the country to exchange their dreams with one another. As he explains his mission: "I was trying to create an alternative scientific community that anyone could participate in by virtue of his being a dreamer, because in effect every dreamer is a researcher, and every dream is an experiment in the consciousness" (this and the above quotation are from "Group Dreaming," Patrick Huyghe, *Omni,* July 1983).

Since the days of the *Sundance Community Dream Journal,* the dreamwork movement has affected the waking and dreaming lives of millions of Americans. A group of former high school classmates in Camden, New Jersey, use dreamwork as a context for keeping in touch with each other. Researchers at Batelle Institute in Columbus, Ohio, trade dreams to stimulate each other's creativity. Cloistered Roman Catholic nuns in Oregon share dreams that comment on their specialized living conditions, as do prisoners in the Florida State penal system.

Sometimes, whole communities engage in group dreamwork. Partially in response to harassment from outside developers and partially out of a desire to strengthen their ties with one another, the houseboat residents of Sausalito, California, shared their dreams from 1977 through 1984. The project was the brainchild of houseboater John Van Damm, who collected contributions through a centrally located "Dream Drop" and then published them in his own mimeographed periodical called *Gates: A Sausalito Waterfront Community Dream Journal*. In a 1983 discussion of the project, Van Damm remarked:

*Evoking the power of dream and giving dream an active role within a community have positive effects on the life of the community. When community members see themselves and their waking life reflected in the dreams of their neighbors, transformations result that affect the total community. As the dream experience serves to renew the individual, so does the community spirit become renewed each time a dream is shared. (from "Community Dream Work," in* Coat of Many Colors, *San Rafael CA: Dream Tree Press, 1983)*

Interest in experimental dreamwork has flourished in other parts of the world as well. In several Israeli kibbutzim, dream-swapping is now a regularly conducted activity, open to all members who keep records of their dreams. In a major hospital in Buenos Aires, Argentina, long-term patients are gaining self-awareness and companionship through exploring one another's dream lives. In a Sydney, Australia, senior citizens' center, residents have organized a dream group to add a note of meaningful exchange to their otherwise rather solitary and tedious weekly schedule. And in London, England, Tony and Hyone Crisp write a regular dream column for the *Daily Mail* featuring dreams sent in by their readers. Ultimately, the Crisps intend to use this body of material as the primary source for a "dream profile" of England.

One of the most fascinating current dreamwork endeavors is based in Tokyo, Japan, where Dr. Randy Morris, an American who teaches at the Hiroshima International School, has been polling *hibakusha* (survivors of the 1945 atomic bomb attacks) and other Japanese citizens for dreams that contain images of nuclear holocaust. Morris's purpose is to chart the efforts of the dreaming psyche to "imagine the unimaginable," in the hope that he can establish the existence of some sort of collective survival mechanism in dreaming. Certain dreams, he believes, may be meant to shock an individual's mind in such a way that he or she is forced to address something that poses a danger to the species. By logical extension, images from such dreams may be useful in alerting others to the danger or in figuring out ways to deal with the danger.

Even in the Soviet Union, experiential dreamwork is finding a niche, albeit a narrow and chilly one. Officially, amateur dreamwork is discouraged and even persecuted, on the grounds that such matters are better left to government research. It's a policy that has never changed and continues to be enforced, despite the *glasnost* trend of the Gorbachev years. Unofficially, however, contemporary Soviet dreamworkers are managing to do what they want to do.

On a recent visit to Moscow, I met with Barbara Ivanova, a deeply committed dream activist who is one of three Soviet subscribers to the *Dream Network Bulletin*. Ivanova had a long and distinguished scientific career as a researcher of psychic phenomena; but when she began arguing in the late 1970s for an ethical code to govern the procedures and applications of parapsychological research (including dream studies), her laboratory was closed and she was forbidden to teach, even in a nonprofessional mode. This official censure meant that she was confined to Moscow, and that her movements within the city would be ever subject to surveillance. Consequently, she must now meet with her Wednesday evening dream group outside the Star Cinema in Moscow, where the group (which calls itself the "Star Academy") can be camouflaged as part of the crowd waiting for the next show. When the group is broken up by the police—a frequent occurrence—members retreat to a nearby park and share dreams in safer small groups of two or three.

What Ivanova goes to such pains to enjoy is, in her words, "the strength and purpose" she derives from examining her own dream life along with the dream lives of other dreamers. In the United States, that strength and purpose is far more easily obtained. At the local level, dream "clubs" ranging in size from five to fifty dreamers typically recruit members by word of mouth or through classified ads, especially ads in campus and free press periodicals. Often these groups are large and open-ended networks, such as the Metro D.C. Dream Community or the Dreamworkers Support Group of San Francisco. Sometimes they are small groups designated only by a person's name and address. On the national level, there are two burgeoning organizations that are designed to serve professional and amateur dreamworkers alike: the Association for the Study of Dreams (P. O. Box 3121, Falls Church, VA 22043) and the Dream Educators Network (P. O. Box 788, Cooperstown, NY 13326).

The Association for the Study of Dreams (ASD) is technically an international group that attempts to bridge the often troubled waters separating the "official" scientific community interested in dreams (which includes neurology specialists and anthropologists as well as psychiatrists and psychologists) and the "unofficial" universe of lay dreamworkers (which includes practicing "dream counselors" as well as private individuals). It publishes a bimonthly newsletter that serves as a forum, but its major activity is an annual, week-long conference held in a different United States city each summer. In 1988, for example, the ASD met in Santa Cruz, California, and offered speeches, symposia, and workshops on such subjects as "The Functions of Dreams and Dreaming Sleep," "Political Night-mares: Dreams of Salvadoran Refugees," and "Women's Bodies, Women's Dreams." The conference concluded, as usual, with a Dream Ball, which all participants were invited to attend in a costume depicting one of their favorite dream characters.

The Dream Educator's Network (DEN) also has international connections; but, like the ASD, its membership is overwhelmingly from the United States. DEN was created especially for profes-sionals or amateurs who are therapists, leaders of dream groups, or public authorities on dream-related matters; but in actuality, any-one can join. With the instigation and direction of individual members, it sponsors numerous "one-shot" projects aimed at al-lowing the participants to share their experiences, dreamwork methods, and career-building strategies. Each year, it publishes an updated *International Directory of Dreamworkers.*

Most of the ideas, examples, and experiments presented in *Night and Day* have evolved from my participation in the dreamwork movement I've just described. Whether you work on your dreams by yourself, with someone else, or in a group, the movement is there to assist you, and it's easy to tap. Other dreams and other dreamers can teach you a great deal about how to bring your own waking and dreaming lives into more powerful harmony. Thanks to the movement, so can *Night and Day.*

# 2

# Getting to Know Your Dreams

ALL DREAMS ARE not created equal. Like individual real-life episodes, they contain different proportions of diamond and rust. Some are predominantly brilliant, witty, or fun, while others are mainly dull, silly, or painful. Unless we take the time to examine our dreams, however, we won't easily be able to make distinctions. All our dreams will seem weird and confusing.

We tend to think that our dreams in general are messier and less rational than our waking life, but this is only superficially true, as careful study of either our waking life or our dream life (and preferably both) will tell us. In John Updike's novel *S.*, the protagonist writes a series of confessional letters to explain her life to the loved ones she has abandoned. Updike comments:

*One of the things I was very aware of in writing the letters is the incongruous mix in our lives of the most grave issues with the barrage of trivia that has to be handled. It's hard to separate the trivia from the big stuff. I think they're all somehow on the same level, in an odd way.*

> *Certainly, as we live from day to day, our shoelaces coming undone and*
> *the fact that we're going to die someday, both occur to us on almost the*
> *same wavelength. (from Mervyn Rothstein, "In 'S.,' Updike Tries the*
> *Woman's Viewpoint,"* New York Times, *March 25, 1988)*

Dreams are much like letters we write to ourselves each night. They exhibit the same odd juxtaposition of the cosmic and the mundane that Updike mentions, and they can vary widely from night to night in content, format, and quality, depending on the mood of our "dream correspondent" self. All dreams merit a second look for what they communicate to us about our state of being; and many of them are also worth some form of analytical scrutiny, be it playful or methodical. A powerful symbol or message may lie concealed in a very simple dream scene, and a little dreamwork may bring it out.

If certain dreams are more significant than others (*i.e.,* can have more potential meaning in our lives), and if appearances can be deceiving, the question then becomes, "How do I tell which dreams are important, or potentially important?" The source of the answer is the same as the source of our dreams: our feelings.

A dream that is especially powerful is almost always accompanied by some sort of sensory signal. In certain cases, the visual images in the dream may be unusually crisp or colorful. If you dream of a forest, for example, you may be struck by the sharp contrast between the deep blue sky and the shimmery green foliage; or you may be attracted to the amazingly intricate design of a wildflower; or you may be impressed by the atypically wide spectrum of hues you see—ochres, magentas, purples, and tans as well as basic primary colors like reds, blues and greens. In other cases, a particular dream event may stimulate a sense that isn't often involved in your dreams. Perhaps you smell gasoline in a dream, taste oranges, feel sand under your feet, or hear a full orchestra playing.

There are many other ways a dream can broadcast its special nature. It can offer you an intensely sensational experience, like a flight to a mountaintop, a narrow escape from death, or a first-place showing in the Boston Marathon. It can give you an unusually attractive gift, like an ancient art object, a rare orchid, or a long-lost childhood toy. It can even make a blatant announcement, like a voice (maybe your own dream voice) proclaiming, "I've found it, the secret to the universe!" When the signal is this strong, you can't always assume that the dream is important in the way it *claims* to be, but you can be sure that it *is* important, since it is obviously connected with strong feelings.

Most dreams offer much more subtle clues to their importance: a general tone or presence that sets them apart from other dreams that may possess similar images and events. Mircea Eliade, the cultural historian, refers to this indicator as "a religious aura." Others call it an echoing or ringing quality. In my own experience, it's more like a "buzz": a half-auditory, half-visceral sensation of mild excitement that is perceptible as an undercurrent in the dream itself or in my reaction to the dream after awakening. Whatever you call the feeling — tingle, click, spark, aha, gotcha, satori — it's in the same class as "gut feeling": imprecise, but recognizable once you start paying attention to your dreams and noting your reactions to them.

We can't pay very good attention to our dreams, however, if we don't remember most of them and if we don't keep track of what we do remember. Before we start looking at how dreamwork experiments can contribute to achieving personal goals, we need to consider some of the methods we can use to improve our dream recall and to record our dreams in an efficient and serviceable manner.

## Remembering Dreams

Waking up under any circumstances shocks the mind, let alone waking up to an electronic wail (whether it's static or a top-forty song) or to the pressures of a day that's largely programmed. If you add to this crisis of consciousness the facts that we don't usually wake up right after dreaming and that we may be slow to reach a state of full alertness, then it comes as no surprise that dreams are so difficult to remember. Chances are good that when we do recall a dream, it's only a fragment from the very end; so if we really want to know what happened in that dream, we have to try to extrapolate everything from that one flimsy piece of evidence.

Dream scholars actually have fun thinking of metaphors for how difficult the challenge of dream recall can get. Ann Faraday, author of *Dream Game* and *Dream Power,* says it can be like attempting to summarize the plot of a mystery novel after reading only the last page. Edwin Kiester, a freelance writer on medical subjects, says we can be "just as baffled on waking as if we had walked into the finale of *Don Giovanni* without witnessing the previous acts." Karen McCoy, leader of the Gate of Horn dream group in Atlanta, refers to the problem at its worst as "having to play charades in absolute darkness randomly interrupted by a strobe light." My favorite metaphor of all comes from Liam Hudson, author of *Night Life,* who claims the task can become so tricky that the dreamer may as well "try to reconstruct the pattern of a Fair Isle sweater from its yarn once it has been unraveled."

It helps to acknowledge that dream recall can often be very difficult, so that we don't set our standards too high. At the same time, we need to remind ourselves that a dream is not as strictly linear as a mystery novel or *Don Giovanni.* Many times, a single clue can evoke the essence of a dream: its emotional underpinning, the probable waking-life references that are being made, and the most likely dream scenario. Such is the power of a dream image. We have to guard against the mistaken logic that suggests we'd remember most of our dreams if dreaming were really important. The same logic tells us that God would have given us wings if we were really meant to fly.

Fortunately, it isn't always difficult to remember dreams. In fact, sometimes it's easy—especially if the dream is a very powerful one, or if we wake up immediately after dreaming, or if we are not obligated the next morning to set our usual routines in motion right after waking. Dream recall is also, luckily, a skill that can be learned.

Here are some steps you can take (separately or in combination) to remember dreams more often and more clearly:

- Tell yourself several times during the day that you intend to remember your dreams, and repeat this intention with particular conviction just before you fall asleep.

- Place an object with a scent—a bag of herbs, a sachet, a room deodorant—near your bed as a "dream enhancer." The fact that you have consciously associated this scent with dreaming may trigger dream recall during the fuzzy moments of waking up.

- Place a pencil and paper (or dream journal) next to your bed to record dream images as soon as you recall them—even in the middle of the night. Just knowing this equipment is there will also predispose you to remember your dreams.

- Drink a glass of water before retiring. It will help you wake up faster or more often.

- Avoid alcohol and drugs before retiring. These substances can suppress REM sleep.

- Set your alarm for an earlier time than usual. You may surprise yourself in the middle of a dream. Over a week or a month, vary the times for which you set your alarm, so that your sleeping life doesn't always conform to the same pattern.

- Before retiring, write down a few lines about what you did and how you felt during the day, with the knowledge that your dreams may comment on these events and feelings. This activity will condition you to want to remember your dreams, so that you can compare them to your state of mind just prior to falling asleep.

■ As soon as you awaken (whether it's in the middle or at the end of your night's sleep), lie still for a minute and concentrate on recalling your dreams. If you can't get anywhere this way, ask yourself how you feel. The best way to recapture a dream that you can't quite remember is to follow your emotions back into it. Images will arise as you explore your feelings, and these images are likely to be the same ones that you dreamed during the night or, if not, to lead you back to your dream images.

   As an alternative to asking yourself about your *feelings,* you can try asking yourself what you're *thinking.* For many people, the line between feeling and thinking is very thin.

■ As soon as you can recall a dream, record it in writing, even if you only jot down a few key words. In the case of an especially remarkable dream image, you may want to make a brief sketch. (See below for more detailed suggestions.)

■ Throughout the following day, be alert to feelings or events that trigger memories of your previous night's dream life. Often you won't remember a dream until you encounter something in your waking life that relates to the dream.

Simply maintaining a curiosity about your dream life—in other words, staying interested in your dreams—is the biggest single step you can take toward improving your dream recall. It's also the major factor in learning how to interpret your dreams. Like a child eagerly listening to his or her parents, you will soon pick up the language of your dreams and give that language meaning through the way you live.

## Recording Dreams

Attending to dreams, as I've already suggested, can give you wonderful training in the language arts. Although you can't expect to recapture an entire dream *as it actually was,* you can try to recreate *what it was like;* and in doing so, you will inevitably develop new, more imaginative ways of expressing your thoughts, feelings, and experiences.

You may surprise yourself with a dream description that not only is beautiful in itself, but also inspires a revelation about the meaning of the dream. A friend of mine once recorded a dream image as "a huge shadow rumbling over me like the ghost of an elephant." Her use of the words "rumbling" and "ghost of an elephant," which were not offered within the dream itself, prompted her to realize that the dream was commenting on her piano lessons. Aside from evoking the resonance of a piano, "rumble" was close to "Trimble," the name of her piano teacher; and "ghost of an elephant" suggested the large "dead" legs of the piano and the ivory keys.

You may even find yourself coining words spontaneously to capture the special flavor of a strange dream detail or occurrence. One dream-recorder I know invented the term "shamster" to denote a recurring character in his dreams who pretends to be docile and sympathetic, but sooner or later reveals himself to be sinister and devious. Another dream-sharing partner created the neologism "snitlock" to describe an incident in one of her dreams when her dream self displayed a peculiarly peevish obsession with a trivial insult. No matter how you choose to pin down your dreams in words, with practice you are bound to become more adept at defining vague feelings and at articulating experiences that partake of the novel and the irrational.

Most dreams are so unusual and so nonverbal that they virtually dare the dreamer to put their images and feelings into words, and it's a dare that the serious dreamworker needs to accept. It's wonderful simply to exercise your verbal creativity through recording your dreams, but what's truly exciting about keeping a dream journal is the opportunity it gives you to make your dreams more intelligible—and, as a result, more useful—to your waking mind.

In addition to functioning as an invaluable aid for remembering your dreams, a dream journal is a vehicle for processing dreams into action. Consider the story of Adam naming the animals, which appears in the Bible as the very first human achievement. The animals may have existed before receiving their names, but it was that act of naming which rendered them knowable to the human mind and, therefore, thinkable. At the beginning of any mindful endeavor is the word.

Some dreamworkers prefer the spoken word to the written word, especially after just waking up, so they recite their dreams into a tape recorder and transcribe them later, at a more convenient time. Most people, however, prefer to write down their dreams as soon as possible after they happen: It takes less total time, even if the resulting entries may not be as thorough as tape transcriptions can be. No matter which approach you take, the end product should be a written dream journal, one that can easily be used as a reference tool.

The more frequently you write down your dreams, and the sooner you record a dream after you have it, the better. It's impossible to judge right away if a dream is going to be valuable to you—that takes a certain amount of wide-awake time and thought. Regrettably, every minute of waking life that goes by after you have a dream generally makes that dream much more difficult to recapture.

I've found that if I take the trouble immediately after awakening to jot down even the most fragmentary impressions that I have of a dream, I can almost always rescue the whole dream from oblivion. Later in the day, more and more material comes back to me about that dream, which is far less often the case if I don't write something down during those first few critical minutes. Mark Barasch, editor of *New Age Journal,* advises:

> *. . . don't disdain even tiny dream fragments. These seemingly random tailings are often a holographic image of the bigger dream; they resemble nothing so much as those freeze-dried hikers' dinners that look like wood-shavings in the bag but, with a little attention, can be brewed into passable Stroganoff. (from "A Hitchhiker's Guide to Dreamland," New Age Journal, October 23, 1983, p. 39)*

Ideally, a dream journal entry should be made as soon after the dream as possible and be as complete as possible; but the ideal does not always fit the real situation. The timing, thoroughness, and complexity of your record-keeping should be in accord with your individual capacities and lifestyle. Otherwise, you may be tempted to abandon record-keeping altogether. Basically, any record is a lot better than none.

Here are some guidelines for recording dreams in a journal:

- Devote an entire journal exclusively to dreams. Most people find that this method permits quicker and more convenient cross-referencing of individual dreams. Some people, however, prefer to incorporate a dream journal into a daily journal, so that they can more easily draw connections between their waking and dreaming lives. If you would rather try the latter approach, devise some means of distinguishing your day entries from your dream entries (such as using pens with different colors of ink, or drawing borders around each dream entry).

- Keep your dream journal next to your bed, where you can reach it without straining. Choose a journal format that is easy to use even while you are lying in bed in the middle of the night. You may prefer a small journal because it's less bulky, or a large journal because it's easier to find and use in the dark, or a clipboard with loose-leaf sheets that you can later insert into a binder.

■ At night, make sure that there are several writing implements at hand, in case one malfunctions, and that the lighting is appropriate for any nighttime entries. It should not be so bright it might cause total wakefulness (especially for a bed partner!) and not so dim that you can't see what you're writing. Some people use a penlight attached to a ball-point pen for writing in the dark. Other people prefer not to turn on a light at all.

■ When you wake up from a dream, lie still and take a few moments to relive the dream in your mind as fully as you can. Then repeat it to yourself verbally before finally writing it down. This will help ensure that you don't forget the dream as you take the time to compose your entry. It will also serve to remind you of how you *felt* during the dream, which often gets overlooked by the waking mind's preoccupation with "who, what, where, when, why."

■ Write down the dream in whatever manner comes automatically. Don't worry about sentence structure or grammar, just concern yourself with recording the dream accurately and completely. Often this may mean just jotting down a few phrases, because you can't be sure what else happened, or how these images were connected. Don't strain to compose a logical, linear, cause-and-effect scenario if it didn't exist in your dream (or, more precisely, in your *memory* of your dream).

■ Don't incorporate any interpretive remarks into the entry itself. Interpretation comes later and may or may not wind up being recorded in your journal, depending on your preference. Some dreamers like to keep their dream journals "pure"—unprejudiced by interpretive remarks, which they store elsewhere.

■ It's a good idea to record a dream in the present tense, as if you were simultaneously experiencing and narrating it. This keeps you focused on what really happened and makes the dream seem more immediate on rereading.

■ Be sure to recount how you feel during the dream as well as what's happening. If you have difficulty describing or even remembering your feelings (a common problem in our Western, technocratic civilization, which tends to devalue feelings), ask yourself questions aimed at recalling your feelings when you were at different stages of the dream: for example, "How did I feel while this event was happening? Was I scared? Was I exhilarated? Was I shivering? Was I warm? Was I awestruck? Was I angry? Was I indifferent?"

You can also make an effort not to lapse into metaphors when you write your feelings down in your journal entry: for example, "I feel like a robot" or "I feel as if I'm in a horror movie." These "intellectualized" metaphors for feelings often go beyond clear description (which you want at this point) to interpretation (which works best if it is a separate process, performed later). One trick that will help you to focus more squarely on your primary emotional and physical feelings rather than your metaphorical feelings is to avoid altogether the phrases "I feel like" or "I feel as if" and try using just the phrase "I am."

■ Over time, you may want to develop a system of codes to use in your dream entries for special purposes. Here are some suggestions:

> Draw a wavy line *between* words to indicate a detail or sequence of the dream that you've forgotten.
> Draw a wavy line *under* a word if it's not quite the right one, but you can't think of a better one.
> Place quotation marks around an image that is not really what it claims to be (for example, "I am sitting in my

'apartment'" [assuming the dream apartment does not correspond to your real apartment]).

Use an oversized X in a circle to indicate an abrupt change in scene.

If you're not certain about the order of events, indicate this by isolating each event in its own circle on the page.

■ Feel free to draw sketches as part of your dream entry. They can be valuable shortcuts for communicating information, plus they may stimulate your memory and imagination in ways that verbal expression may not. Floor plans or maps serve to indicate direction and flow of movement more efficiently and comprehensively than prose. Pictures of significant objects and patterns can be especially revealing when it comes time to interpret your dream.

■ Give the dream a title. The first idea that comes to you is usually the best, since it is likely to capture your basic response to the dream. Otherwise, create a title around one of the major images in the dream, preferably the most exotic one. The title will help fix the dream in your memory and will also function as a reference aid.

■ Date the dream for easy reference. For the sake of clarity, use the morning-after date for overnight dreams.

■ Note any memorable circumstances surrounding the dream event itself. You might note, for example, whether it woke you up, whether a bed partner heard you cry out, or whether you had the dream right after turning off the alarm clock and falling back to sleep.

■ Leave wide margins around, and some room after, each entry for later insertions, such as further memories of the dream or subsequent dreamwork comments. If you adopt the habit of always beginning a dream entry at the top of a page, you can most often accomplish this purpose, and your dream journal will be easier to review.

■ When traveling, leave your dream journal at home so that you don't risk losing it (and so that your luggage will be lighter!). Record your away-from-home dreams on loose sheets of paper. If you use only one side of each sheet, and the sheets themselves are not quite as big as the sheets in your journal, then you can tape or staple these loose sheets into your journal when you return, so that your away-from-home dreams will follow the previous dreams in the right order.

If the trip away from home is a long, leisurely one, you may want to take your journal with you and do some extensive dream-reviewing. In such a situation, it's good for security's sake to put your name and either your address or your phone number inside the journal's cover; however, you may decide that you don't want a stranger (or a friend or family member, for that matter) to be able to link your name to such an intimate document.

## Reviewing Your Dream Journal

Keeping a dream journal is beneficial in itself. Since it compels you to linger over your dreams as you write them down, the odds are greater that your dreams will wind up being stored in your long-term memory. Most of the value of keeping a dream journal, however, lies in reviewing it from time to time. Only then can you get a good sense of the overall quality of your dream life and how it influences, and is influenced by, the quality of your waking life. This insight can be a critical element in using dreams to achieve your goals, as we'll see in the chapters that follow.

Try to be methodical in reviewing your journal. Set a schedule for reviewing your dreams that is appropriate to the volume of dreams in your journal: anywhere from once a week (assuming you have at least three or four recorded dreams in this period), to once a month, to once every six weeks (which is a reasonable outside limit if you want to remain in touch with your dream life).

In addition to their other review times, many dreamworkers make it a point to read through their dream journals on certain special occasions, like their birthday, New Year's Day, summer vacation, or the spring and fall equinoxes. One amateur stargazer I know schedules his periodic review for the days surrounding each full moon. Adding an element of ceremony to your review—either on a regular or an occasional basis—can help make the whole process more attractive, impressive, and memorable.

The object of a dream journal review is to establish any patterns among your dreams: recurrent characters, plots, themes, locales, objects, behaviors, or emotions. You can either note these patterns mentally as you read through your journal or keep track of the patterns using a checklist. In general, this activity will bring to light the subjects and feelings that are most dominant in your dream life and, therefore, worth examining in your waking life as well. Specific suggestions for recording dream image patterns and for applying this knowledge to dreamwork are included in the following chapters.

You may also want to chart dreams that fall into particular categories, such as:
- nightmares
- psychic dreams (dreams that either seemed at the time, or later proved to be, telepathic or precognitive in nature)
- active versus passive dreams (dreams defined according to your role in determining the course of events)
- wish-fulfillment dreams (dreams in which you experience a secret desire)
- flying dreams (dreams in which you yourself—perhaps with some magic assistance—are the flying agent)
- lucid dreams (dreams in which you are conscious that you are dreaming *while* you are dreaming)

- false awakening dreams (dreams in which you think you have woken up, and then come to realize that you're still dreaming)
- out-of-the-body dreams (dreams in which you appear to leave your body, and can see it from an exterior vantage point)
- physiological dreams (dreams in which you feel an unusually strong body sensation, like warmth, coldness, the desire to urinate, thirst, or hunger)
- wise old dreams (dreams during which you feel you've learned a lesson)

As you continue to review your dream journal, you'll acquire whole new worlds of information about who you are and what makes you tick; and eventually you'll create your own uniquely meaningful categories. For example, one member of my dream group suddenly realized during a review of her dream journal that she was indeed fascinated with the backs of people's necks, both in her dream life and in her waking life. Now it's a formal category in her review. Contributors to the *Dream Network Bulletin* often discuss the dream subjects that hold special interest for them, including a nature-lover who keeps track of hawk dreams because the hawk is his favorite or "totem" animal, a baseball pitcher who is doubly attentive to any dream in which he's throwing something, and a computer analyst who collates (on her computer, of course) every dream she has that relates to computer hardware, software, programming, or logic systems.

I like to collect dream puns. An example is an image from one of my recent dreams that baffled me for weeks: A bunch of my friends were kneeling around the carpet in my living room and hacking it to pieces with long, pointed scissors. I enjoyed watching them do this and couldn't figure out why. Was I a masochist? I asked myself. Finally, when I reviewed my dream journal a couple of weeks later, I saw that I'd dreamed of my grandmother's house, where I'd spent a lot of time as a child, several times that month, including the same night I'd had my carpet dream. It struck me in a flash that my friends had been *dancing* in that dream. My grandmother had often used the expression "cut a rug" for dancing and it had fascinated me as a child. Not knowing what it really meant, I had taken it at face value and had thought it was a neat thing for people to do to have fun.

This flash of understanding I got from reviewing my dream journal suddenly made that particular dream much more intelligible. It also made me wonder how many of our unusual dream images, especially punning images, date to our preliterate childhood, when we were confused about the meaning of words or expressions, or when we made no distinction among words with similar phonetic properties. At any rate, I have a category for dreams of this type that I call "kiddie hangovers." It includes a Christmastime dream that features the mysterious appearance in Bethlehem of a fat man named "Round John Vershun" and a foggy dream where I find myself in the "mist" of my enemies.

The next step after having, remembering, recording, and reviewing a dream is to interpret it. Complicated as this may sound, it's actually a very easy, smoothly flowing, almost automatic process. Nevertheless, it's important to distinguish each of these stages in coming to terms with a dream, because so many people rush from having a dream to interpreting it. In doing so, they skip the critical "incubation" period that gives the dream ample opportunity to speak for itself.

Without first taking some time to make sure we recall a dream as vividly and faithfully as we can, and then taking some more time to relive and ponder that dream, we risk making only superficial judgments about what that dream could mean. Such judgments are ultimately unsatisfying for two reasons. First, we've missed the full adventure of learning something new. Instead, like so many misguided students today who feel pressured to produce a "right" answer, we've slapped a quick-fix solution on something that puzzles us. Second, those superficial judgments about the dream's meaning can work unfairly to make the entire dream appear super-ficial. Once fixed in our minds, they can function as obstacles to any richer understanding of the dream.

The next chapter discusses ways in which we can interpret our dreams so that we can enjoy the full benefit of what they have to offer us. With just a little care, we can help any dream retain its hold on our imagination and its power to affect our destiny in a positive, inspirational manner.

# 3

# Interpreting Your Dreams

N THEIR STUDIES of the human mind, experts generally learn more from observing defective mental functioning than they do from observing normal or superior mental functioning. Such was the experience of Oliver Sacks, the renowned American neurologist, when he worked with a teenage client he calls Rebecca.

When Sacks first met Rebecca, her verbal clumsiness, her repeated incapacity to follow simple instructions, and her abysmal performance on IQ tests seemed to confirm what people had always said about her: that she was a moron, an idiot, a fool. Nevertheless, Sacks gradually discovered another dimension of Rebecca's mental life that profoundly impressed him. She responded with unusual sensitivity to the intricate liturgy, prayers, and rites of Orthodox Judaism. She loved to hear stories and poems and demonstrated a keen understanding of even highly sophisticated metaphorical language. At moments of great sorrow or joy, she would burst forth with beautiful symbolic images to express herself. And then there were her dreams, which proved to be especially vivid and important to her after her beloved grandmother died, and which she communicated to Sacks with skill and animation.

What was Sacks to make of this enigmatic mind, so inept in one respect and yet so powerful in another? The answer came to him with the blinding force of revelation: Rebecca was a "narrative" being. She relied strictly on narrative, symbolic modes to give her world coherence, rather than on pattern-seeking, problem-solving, logical modes. In this respect, Sacks decided, she was like all of us are as children:

> *Very young children love and demand stories, and can understand complex matters presented as stories, when their powers of comprehending general concepts, paradigms, are almost non-existent. It is this narrative or symbolic power which gives a* sense of the world—*a concrete reality in the imaginative form of symbol and story*—*when abstract thought can provide nothing at all. (from Sacks,* The Man Who Mistook His Wife for a Hat, *New York: Harper & Row, 1987, pp. 183–184* [emphasis is his])

In my opinion, dreams are a product of that narrative part of our being which is struggling to make sense of our continually mysterious experience. Psychologists tell us (and some of us remember) that as children, we were very attuned to our dreams. As adults, however, we put most of our faith and energy into functional or rational knowledge; consequently, the kind of poetic knowledge we express in our dreams tends to go unheeded and unappreciated. Our dreams no longer make as much "sense" to us, because we have been conditioned by social pressures to associate "sense" with what is rational, with what everyone can agree is "real."

To get back in touch with our dreams is to become more aware of our private sense of things, our personal truths, the story lines that we have spun in an effort to make order out of chaos. Because most of us have evolved into predominantly "rational" beings, we now need formal dream interpretation processes—at least in the beginning—to re-establish this vital connection.

Like the myths that convey the true spirit of a culture in a way that its factual history cannot, our dreams speak for our lives in a way that our factual biographies cannot. Myths and dreams alike are concerned with the transcendent essence of what it is to be human, so they engage in a mode of discourse that is far different from the information-sharing speech we use to meet our day-to-day survival needs. And because they speak differently, they demand a different mode of attention. In the words of the famous American psychologist Erich Fromm: "Both dreams and myths are important communications from ourselves to ourselves. If we do not understand the language in which they are written, we miss a great deal of what we know and tell ourselves in those hours when we are not busy manipulating the outside world."

The language to which Fromm refers, the language of myths as well as dreams, is the language of symbols. The goal of dream interpretation is to gain more insight into our personal symbols—the images, feelings, and narratives that operate at the very core of who we are and how we live.

Briefly defined, a symbol is an image that has a special meaning. Some symbolic images are realistic in appearance but are understood to stand for something greater, to represent complex ideas, feelings, or entities in a simpler, more tangible and immediate way. On a collective level, there's the image of a wooden cross to symbolize Christianity; a star-spangled, red-and-white-striped flag to symbolize the United States; or an apron to symbolize mother. On a personal level, such an image may be a scarlet maple leaf to symbolize football season in your Midwestern hometown, the logo of your local tavern to symbolize escape from pressure, or a melting icicle to symbolize the end of a wintertime love affair in your present or past.

Other symbolic images are "invented" realities. They attempt to describe ideas, feelings, or entities that are not otherwise apparent, tangible, or even conceivable in rational terms by relating them to things that are—even if those things do not actually exist in the world as we know it. On a collective level, there's the image of a vampire to symbolize the perplexing and monstrous capability that certain people possess to victimize others; or a talking convertible to symbolize the way an automobile can sometimes seem to have a will of its own. On a personal level, such an image may be a magical house with ever-expanding rooms and hallways to symbolize a new lifestyle that offers you more personal freedom; or a coworker dressed as Pee Wee Herman to symbolize a bizarre, childlike quality about that person which your conscious mind has not yet been able to articulate.

A final class of symbolic images is best described as playful (and, as a consequence, mentally challenging) counter-representations. One image stands in place of another image because it has something in common with it. On a collective or a personal level, this type of symbolic expression can take the form of a straightforward metaphorical association (such as comparing a cave to a pocket, snoring to sawing logs, a pumpkin to a coach, a head of hair to a forest) or it can take the form of a more obscure riddle or pun (such as chopping shrubbery for refusing to be specific—"beating around the bush"—or heavy-breathing mallards for ventilation ducts).

## Decoding Dream Symbols

Given that dreams are symbolic narratives, how do we go about translating what individual dream images represent? Dream symbol dictionaries abound in libraries, bookstores, and supermarkets. Look under "aardvark" in any one of them and you may find that it means you have a craving for something exotic and animal in your love life; or that you're about to be visited by a flamboyant, large-nosed stranger; or that an authority figure with an accent has a lot of "'ard vork" for you to do. How are you to know which interpretation fits your dream, or if any of them fits, or if all of them fit to some degree?

Only you, the dreamer—not a dream dictionary or any other outside source—can determine what the images in your dream mean. These images are derived from your individual experience and, therefore, they have very personal connotations. Because each human life is unique, the set of possible meanings an aardvark has for you is bound to differ considerably from the set of possible meanings an aardvark has for someone else. More than this, a dream image acquires a great deal of its specific meaning from its context, that is, its relationship to the other images in the same dream. The proper question, then, is not "What does an aardvark mean when it appears in a dream?" but rather "Among all the other images stored in my mind, why did I dream of an aardvark? What makes it an appropriate image for this particular dream?"

While dream dictionaries are completely useless as direct translating media, they can start us thinking about possible directions to take when we're pursuing the meaning of various kinds of imagery in our dreams. Like observing how someone else draws to improve our own drawing, looking through dream dictionaries (especially the more discursive "dream-dictionary" sections of full-length books on dreams) can help us develop greater flexibility and imagination in arriving at our own symbolic interpretations. This is especially true in the case of those images that are known by report to be common to the dreams of most dreamers.

Purely for illustrative purposes, I offer the following sampling of some of the more common dream images together with a brief list of what several different dream dictionaries have to say about them:

## Accident

- a desire to punish yourself or a perception of yourself as "self-punishing"

- a perception of yourself as incompetent or "dangerous to yourself or others"
- a feeling that a certain life situation is getting out of control
- a desire to resolve dramatically some anger or fear
- a distrust of whatever elements contribute to that accident (for example, if the accident occurs in a car, you may be skeptical about your automobile or technology in general)

## Death

- an indication of the end of a particular event or phase in your life and the transition to another event or phase
- a wish to be rid of some element in your behavior or some situation in your present life
- a testing of your fear of death, or rather, a testing of how you'll react to death
- a perception that you have reached some sort of limit in a type of behavior or life situation beyond which you don't know how to go
- a call to fight for your survival in some way
- a signal that some outmoded part of you has to die
- a wish to connect with a higher wisdom or with someone who has died
- a desire for uninterrupted rest or peace

## Falling

- a fear that you are losing your balance in some life situation
- a fear that you are losing status in some respect

- a perception that you are taking a "plunge into the un-known" in some aspect of your life
- an inner excitement or turmoil associated with some major emotional challenge (such as love)
- a feeling of not knowing where you are, of not having any "ground under your feet"
- a wish to escape "upright" adult responsibilities and descend to the ground-oriented world of the child or the animal
- a fear of giving in to pleasure

## Flowers and Plants

- a sense of the beauty that exists in certain aspects of your life
- a feeling of love and tenderness about something in your life
- a sense that you need curative medicine for some illness— physical or situational—in your life (since most medicines come from plants)
- a signal that you are concerned in some way with your genitals (since many flowers exhibit their own reproductive parts so prominently and since many of these parts resemble human male and female reproductive organs)
- a wish to get closer to nature or the more "natural" aspects of your life
- a desire to display a hidden talent
- a feeling that your efforts have "borne fruit"
- an acceptance of the natural cycle, including death
- a perception about a particular group of people in your life, about people in general, or about life in general (assuming that you dream of a mass of vegetation or a landscape covered with natural vegetation)

## Nakedness

- a perception that you are very vulnerable, ill-prepared, or exposed
- a wish to be more self-revealing, to shed burdensome conventions
- a desire for more sensual engagement with your surroundings (for example, if you are naked and in the company of another person, you may want to become more intimate with that person; if you are naked at an office meeting, you may want such meetings to be more personally interesting or involving)
- a feeling that you are guilty, that you have something to hide
- a sense that you are less civilized, more infantile or primitive, than you should be
- a desire to be treated like a baby or a fool in order to punish yourself, to get more attention, or to eliminate the expectation on the part of other people that you should behave like a responsible adult

## Water

- a feeling regarding sex, defined according to the dream circumstances (for example, if you are taking a delightful swim in a moonlit river, you may be experiencing sexual satisfaction in some aspect of your life or you may seek such satisfaction; if you are furiously chopping ice off your freezer wall, you may be experiencing sexual frustration or you may fear such frustration)

- a signal that you are facing a highly emotional situation, one in which your feelings are unsettled, or "liquid," or "in suspension"
- a fear that you are, in effect, "out of your element" in some aspect of your life or that you are "flooded," "swamped," "treading water," or "drowning"
- a sense that certain life situations are now very fluid, subject to change
- a perception that certain life situations are now very messy

What we see in these very general dream-image definitions are examples of the act of symbol interpretation and nothing more. Clearly if you are a lifeguard, or live along a coast, or regularly clean a fish tank, "water" will have a specialized meaning for you that a generic dream-dictionary definition of "water" could not possibly take into account. If you were recently involved in a car accident, then you have a unique field of reference that applies to "accidents," encompassing the time when that particular accident happened, what happened before, what happened after, the place where that particular accident happened, other places in your experience that are like that place, and so on.

When it comes to the specific images that appear in your dreams, you must perform the act of symbol interpretation for yourself. In deciding what each image means, you may certainly consider what other people suggest such an image means, but ultimately there are only three reliable sources of information about it:

- your own waking-life thoughts, feelings, and experiences relevant to that image
- your overall dream-life thoughts, feelings, and experiences relevant to that image
- the other images in that particular dream, and the thoughts, feelings, and experiences that they appear to be communicating

## A Basic Process of Dream Interpretation

The succeeding chapters of this book offer numerous experiments that will help you to translate your dreams. Such an activity involves not only deciphering the meaning of individual dream images, but also carrying the wisdom of your dreams into your waking life. Right now, however, I'd like to present a case-history example of my own basic dream interpretation process as a way of suggesting how to apply the guidelines I've recommended so far.

Here is my dream-journal transcript of a recent, especially memorable dream, written the morning after I experienced the dream:

### The Heartbreak Kid

*I'm being conducted by a guide through a long hall on a foreign planet where things are being tested or rehearsed that resemble things on Earth. Some of these things are well-crafted, but they are all slightly askew. I'm both fascinated and upset by this. For example, the lighting in the hall is meant to look like sunlight, but it has a strange electrical sheen to it. A steam locomotive snakes along the floor without a track. A small black boy pushes a child Scarlett O'Hara on a sled with rubbery runners. Snow falls in masses instead of drops.*

*I end up in a nook where two little girls and a little boy are beating with sticks on what looks like a wooden armchair. The resulting sound entrances me. I realize this must be how they really do make music on this planet—not an Earth-related exhibition—and that these three kids are in school. One little girl obstructs the other two kids: sitting on the chair, putting her tongue out, and causing them to fumble and play badly when their teacher isn't around. I berate her as if I were her teacher.*

*The real teacher comes up and I explain what's happened. The child is expelled even though I can tell the real teacher doesn't believe me and is inclined to defend the girl. As the child is about to be led off, she reaches*

> *up to me with a packet of pretty, hand-drawn cards in her hand. I'm*
> *surprised that she's offering this packet to me and refuse it indignantly.*
> *Then I see her going to throw it out, her only choice, no one wants it,*
> *and it represents her time here. My heart breaks. I want to call her back.*

After recording this dream in my journal, I spent approximately twenty minutes working toward an interpretation of it. Sometimes, hours or even days go by before I get around to working on a dream; but I try to do it within twenty-four hours, so that the sensations I had during the dream are still fairly fresh.

I don't follow a strictly linear, step-by-step procedure in interpreting my dreams, but I do try to keep a certain order to the sequence of my thoughts. Here is an outline of that process as applied to the dream I've just recounted:

**1. Identify initial feelings and impressions about the dream in general.**

I was sure this dream was an important one because that final feeling of sudden grief, despair, and pity (which I automatically thought of as heartbreak) was so intense it literally woke me up. Despite the obvious pain of this feeling, however, I enjoyed the simple experience of being rocked by emotion. It was almost voluptuous. I recognized that this dream, whatever else it was doing, was definitely challenging or exercising my capacity to feel things. It was shaking me up.

The most impressive single element in the dream was the small, misbehaving girl. She seemed positively demonic when I first encountered her. I was certain I was right to discipline her; and yet, was I? I was left wondering what was right and what was wrong and feeling that somehow I'd been bamboozled.

**2. Focus on the major images, actions, and feelings in the dream. Establish any general patterns that exist. Describe the general "shape" of the narrative.**

I carefully established that the major images, actions, and feelings in the dream were: being conducted down the hall, being fascinated and upset, the strange lighting, the snaking locomotive, the boy pushing the child Scarlett O'Hara on the sled, the three kids beating music on the chair, being entranced with the music, the demonic girl's trouble-making, being angry at her, berating her, the teacher expelling the girl though doubting me, the girl offering the pictures, being indignant, refusing the pictures, the girl going to throw the pictures out, being heartbroken.

Among the general patterns in the dream were these:

- recurring examples of imperfect artworks (with a fleeting exposure to a "perfect" artwork, the music)
- lots of "combinations of opposites," such as the electric sunlight, the snaking (animal) locomotive (machine), the three musicians (good and bad), my mixed feeling of indignation and compassion
- several instances of people being moved rather than moving, including my being conducted down the hall, the child Scarlett O'Hara being pushed, the two good kids being frustrated in their music-making, the little girl being expelled, even my being "moved" emotionally without moving to prevent the girl from throwing away her pictures

The general shape, or flow, of the narrative seemed to be this: At first, I'm very detached from things and the things are artificial— they're straining to be real but they aren't. There comes a point, however, when I get involved in what's going on. First, I'm entranced by music and then I get furious at one of the music-makers who starts misbehaving, the demonic girl. I even interact with her. I have strong feelings now, which I try to channel into strong behavior. But ultimately, I completely lose my cool. By the end of the dream, I'm one big, quivering mass of feeling.

3. **Note any correspondences between individual images, actions, feelings, and patterns in your dream and images, actions, feelings, and patterns in your waking life over the last few days.**

All during the week before the dream, I had been busily working on a book about storytelling. Most of the correspondences I was able to establish between my waking life and the dream related to this endeavor. In my book, I was writing as if I were guiding my readers through a strange world—which meant, of course, that I had to imagine myself as my reader, being conducted through a strange world. As always, I was being very judgmental and critical about what I was writing as I was writing it.

Although the individual "exhibits" in the dream didn't correspond one to one with any stories I was telling in the book, they were much like them in that stories are essentially artificial creations. The little black boy might very well have been inspired by a statue I'd seen the day before: one of those old hitching posts made to look like a black servant. It had caused me to ponder issues of fairness, justice, and prejudice, giving me complicated, painful feelings similar to some of the feelings I had in the dream.

In many respects the most intriguing correspondence to my waking life involved the wooden armchair. The chair in which I sit to type is a Commodore chair, a wooden armchair. This realization made me draw a connection between "beating sticks to make music" and "pounding keys to make fluent prose." In my waking-life writing effort, as in the dream, I was experiencing a wide range of emotions (including a deliberately cultivated lack of emotion).

4. **Note any correspondences between individual images, actions, feelings, and patterns in your dream and anything having to do with your past or your ongoing interests.**

As a child, I loved the Bizzaro world in Superman comics. Bizzaro is a parallel Earth where everything is slightly wrong. I felt that the content of my dream (which was filled with children) was influenced by my childhood interest in this concept.

I could relate my journey through the hall and then my confrontation with the young girl to the kind of experience I generally have when I travel abroad: feeling disconnected, noticing how things are not quite like what they are at home, then having some sort of breakthrough event when I start to get involved in the foreign culture, then being slightly heartbroken when I have to leave.

I like the works of the American painter Edward Hopper, and the strange lighting reminded me of the type of light that pervades so many of these works, which tend to communicate isolation and emptiness.

5. **Note any correspondences between individual images, actions, feelings, and patterns in your dream and images, actions, feelings, and patterns in the culture as a whole.**

The Scarlett O'Hara character is an American icon, representing a complex individual who is both a perennial, mischievous child and a strong-willed, pragmatic adult. I felt that her presence in the dream not only underscored the importance of the misbehaving child image that comes later, but also served to represent contrasting aspects of myself.

Sticking with this image, I noticed the cultural stereotypings implicit in a nameless black's serving a name-bearing white, a vigorous male's serving a passive female.

I also thought of common beliefs in our culture: that children in school tend to misbehave in order to get attention; that all adults seem to be (and even should be) "teachers" to children; that the drumbeat is a basic, primitive rhythm akin to the heartbeat.

6. **Note any correspondences between individual images, actions, feelings, and patterns in your dream and images, actions, feelings and patterns in other dreams or in your dream life in general.**

I frequently have "movie-making" or "backstage dreams," and I usually find that they have something to do with my writing. Also, I often dream of child/adult pairs. I could recall one dream right away in which an adult stranger tried to teach me-as-a-child by mirroring my bad behavior, by giving me an object lesson. It seemed that something like that was happening in this dream, only reversed.

7. **Based upon all the information you've accumulated by now, determine what you feel the dream is communicating to you about your waking life.**

At this stage of dream interpretation, I try to articulate the full range of possible meanings the dream scenario might contain. Then I test each possible meaning against my feelings, that is, the emotional and sometimes even physical responses triggered by my intuition. Those automatic reflexes usually tell me right away whether a specific possibility is on or off the mark. I begin the testing process by asking myself one basic question: "Aside from the fact that this possible interpretation ties things together, does it move me in any special way? Does it strike a chord? Does it ring a bell?"

Often I won't be able to come up with *specific* judgments regarding what aspects of my waking life are being symbolized by individual dream images and, therefore, what those images are communicating about their waking-life counterparts. Nevertheless, I can always develop a *general* sense of what aspects of my waking life are being addressed by a dream and what that dream is trying to say about them. By comparing this dream information to other feelings, thoughts, and impressions, I inevitably gain more insight into those aspects of my waking life.

Sifting through the mass of images and feelings in my "Heartbreak Kid" dream, I came up with the following possible meanings:

- Anger may be cleansing for me: It may be a pathway to caring about people and issues more deeply. I was so impressed by my anger at the demonic child that I made a special effort to derive some meaning from it. This meaning "rang true," plus it struck me as an especially powerful and sensible idea for me to put into action in my waking life, where I was experiencing anger at certain people that I wasn't expressing. Thus, the fact that I could make good use of this meaning influenced me to accept it.

When you're trying to establish what a dream means, it's important to remember that a possible meaning of a dream is not necessarily some secret message buried inside the dream that helped cause the dream to take shape. A possible meaning of a dream may be an effect of the dream—an intriguing idea that the dream causes you to formulate, once you start comparing that dream to your waking life.

■ I should not intervene in situations when I don't have the authority to do so. This is another possible meaning I could derive from my experience of disciplining the demonic child. After all, I was not the child's teacher, I was only a visitor to the planet, and my action led to painful emotions. Although this meaning appears to contradict the spirit of the previous meaning I discussed, that fact alone would not disqualify it from having lesser, equal, or greater value. Our waking lives certainly present us with situations that have multiple meanings, some contradictory to others, and so do our dreams.

Ultimately, however, I decided to reject this possible meaning for my "Heartbreak Kid" dream. In testing it against my reliving of the dream, it simply didn't feel right. I wasn't ambivalent about berating the child when I did it, and reviewing the dream as a whole, I was very grateful for the insight that resulted from that action.

■ If I categorically reject a "gift" (my own or someone else's), I will suffer heartbreak. This possible meaning instantly struck me as valid. I realized that a major element contributing to my heartbreak was the fact that I turned the child down or, rather, that I felt compelled—for consistency's sake—to turn the child down. Since the child had symbolic importance both as a stranger and as a part of myself, I could interpret the packet of pictures both as an offering from someone else and as a talent or possession that part of myself has to offer.

■ I'm confused about what's real and what's not, and I need to come to terms with this confusion. I was tempted to attach this meaning to the dream for a number of reasons. The dream did expose me to images that were a confusing mixture of reality and fantasy. Also, it's a prevailing concern in late twentieth-century Western culture to wonder what is real and what is not. Finally, I was working on a book dealing with fairy tales, myths, and legends, where the issue of reality versus fantasy is central and frequently controversial.

Nevertheless, my feelings told me that my dream wasn't saying that I was confused about what's real and what's not. Throughout the dream, I was acutely sensitive to, and accurate about, what was real and what was not. In fact, by considering this possible meaning I grew to appreciate that the dream may have been telling me that I was *too* critical about making distinctions between "real" and "not real." If I had been more relaxed about such matters in the dream, I might have enjoyed the bizarre replications (the strange lighting, the snaking locomotive, the rubbery sled, and the clumpy snow) for what they were worth, instead of slightly resenting them. And I might have interacted more constructively—and less dogmatically—with the demonic child.

■ I should try to be more patient with others, and with the misbehaving part of me. I immediately felt that this possible meaning had merit. Part of my heartbreak had been the wish that I had come to know the demonic child better. I also felt that the demonic child represented both other people (who can be disturbing simply because they are "other" than me) and that "other" part of myself that I'm inclined to berate and disavow because it is not in harmony with the outside world.

■ Living by the rules is dangerous and counterproductive. I derived this possible meaning from several elements in the dream. I felt that the various bizarre replications in the dream suffered from the fact that they were straining so hard to repeat the "rules" laid down by the originals. I also felt that the disruptive activity of the child may have been symbolizing how the making of "perfect" music is a doomed effort, perhaps one that encourages madness (symbolized by the child's lack of control). And, finally, I felt that my condemnation of the child for not following the rules somehow backfired: I lost the opportunity to see a precious—and very human—work of art.

Although I sensed that the dream did have this meaning for me, I did not feel it was a meaning of major importance, *i.e.,* a meaning upon which I should base some waking-life action. Instead, I took it as an interesting idea that I should ponder.

■ The wild streak in me that is hard to tame when I write may cause me a great deal of frustration, but it may prove to be the source of my most moving work. As I mentioned before, I identified strongly with the demonic child. Because it "clicked" for me that the "pounding-on-the-chair" music represented my writing efforts, I could also easily accept the notion that the demonic child symbolized my repressed desire to cry out from the gut, rather than to take pains casting what I had to say into civilized, commercially viable language. When I added these impressions to the fact that I was so curious about the demonic child's "packet of pictures" (a good symbolic image for a book), I had no trouble deciding that this meaning was a very potent one to associate with this particular dream.

■ Interactions with people are bound to cause some degree of pain if I expect perfection or demand consistency. Significantly, the only human interaction I experienced in the dream was with the demonic child. Because this specific human interaction in itself was such a singular activity in a relatively cosmic dream (a dream about exploring a planet), and because it was so overwhelmingly consequential, I was forced to consider that it might symbolize some aspect of my human interactions in general.

Maybe, I thought, my dream was reflecting the fact that interactions with people are bound to cause some degree of pain if I
expect perfection or demand consistency. When I tested this
possible meaning first against the feelings and images in my
dream and then against similar feelings and images in my waking
life, it rang true.

■ All human beings are valuable for what they have to communicate about their personal experience of life. Again, I drew a
general meaning from a specific example. Like the demonic child
in my dream, we all have personal "packets of pictures" that
represent our time on Earth. When the child offered me her
packet, I was suddenly awakened to her value as an individual;
and so I determined that the dream was communicating the fact
that everyone has some worthwhile story to tell, no matter how
much we may be tempted to downgrade that individual.

I've already stated that a single dream can yield a multitude of
meanings, some of them contradictory, but I usually like to orches-
trate all or most of those meanings into a single interpretive over-
view. This effort helps me to structure my impressions about a
dream in such a way that I can take positive action in my daily life
based on those impressions.

To facilitate this final step in interpreting "The Heartbreak Kid,"
I returned to the question I asked myself immediately after I had
the dream: Was I right in behaving the way I did with the demonic
child? One choice was to conclude that I handled the situation
poorly. I should have intervened more constructively. At the very
least, I should have accepted the packet of pictures that she offered
me. The other choice was to conclude that I handled the situation
well. However sadly things turned out, I was right to get mad at
the child for maliciously wrecking the beautiful music. In fact, my
harsh treatment of her may well have been the catalyst in getting
her to put forth her own art (the packet of pictures). My strong
emotion at that point in the dream woke me up, but had the dream

continued, I could have—and most likely would have—redeemed her or her art or both.

On the basis of my feelings about the dream, I could make a case for either a "yes" or a "no" answer to my question. Therefore, I decided against the idea that the dream was depicting right or wrong behavior. Instead, I decided that the dream was helping me to realize that I can exercise my power of choice at virtually any stage in a given situation—that I should never act as if I have no choice when I do, which is how I acted in the dream when I refused to accept the demonic child's packet, and (I suddenly realized) how the child acted when she went to throw it away.

At the end of this particular interpretive process, I was left not with a clear statement telling me what I should do, but rather with the haunting image of a young girl holding out a packet of pictures. This image, like any powerful symbol, can never be completely reduced to words, but the effort I made to understand its meaning has fixed it in my mind forever. There it functions as a warning and a hope whenever I'm inclined to shut off parts of myself from others—or from other parts of my self—out of sheer obstinacy.


## Living the Life of Your Dreams

Many people never get involved with dreamwork because they assume that it's a passive enterprise and they prefer more action-oriented enterprises. There's no denying that the process of interpreting a dream is a mental and emotional one, not a physical one. It requires an active commitment to immersing yourself in your dreams, but it's essentially an exercise in allowing the material in your dreams to manifest itself, while you hold your restlessness in check and keep all your rational and imaginative faculties alert and focused.

There's also no denying that dreamwork is preceded by sleeping, which at least *appears* to be a passive state. In fact, dreams testify that the mind is very energetic in this state. Later on, after I've discussed how you can profit from the dreams that come to you spontaneously, I'll outline some ways in which you can take a more active role in programming your dreams so that they stand a better chance of addressing specific problems you want to solve and creative challenges you want to meet. One of the main techniques of this type, known as "dream induction," involves planning what you want to dream and then influencing your mind to produce the desired dream. Another technique of this type, known as "lucid dreaming," involves the possibility of literally directing your dreams with your conscious mind while you are sleeping.

Nevertheless, despite the fact that dreaming in itself is being very active and despite the fact that there are active measures you can take on certain occasions to engineer your dreams, the process of dream interpretation is one of sitting still and playing with puzzles. The dreamwork-scoffers are right: It's not a day in the gym.

Where the dreamwork-scoffers are wrong is in their assumption that dreamwork ends with dream interpretation. The purpose of dreamwork is to equip yourself to function in the world more productively. After interpreting a dream, you need to ask, "How can I translate this dream into action?" The rest of *Night and Day* will show you many ways you can act on your dreams to achieve your waking-life goals.

# 4

# *Dreams and Self-fulfillment*

HEN I WAS ten years old, my parents gave me a toy printing press. Over a wintry weekend of mild sickness and colossal boredom, I published a newsletter based on the only live story at hand: myself. My cold was the subject of the lead article, which I termed "a report from the chest." There were subsequent reports from the brain, the stomach, the muscles, and the heart. For years, this journalistic conceit shaped my moments of introspection, until I matured enough to appreciate that my real "self" was more complex and inscrutable than the sum of the events I'd experienced, the skills and attributes I'd developed, and the facts, opinions, and preferences I'd accumulated.

Take a moment to play a more adult version of this childhood fantasy, one that relates equally well to our culture's obsession with celebrity. Imagine that you have been invited to describe yourself on global TV. You are perfectly comfortable and eager to tell the truth to an adoring and uncritical audience of four billion people. What do you say?

According to a 1981 study on "self-imaging" supervised by Dr. Gerald Clease, a behavorial scientist at the University of Chicago, our first reaction when we are asked to define ourselves is to assume the point of view of an outside observer. Given this perspective, most of the words and categories we wind up using have a socially specific significance: "I'm an American," I'm the mother of three daughters," "I'm a city person," "I'm shy," "I'm a Sagittarius," "I teach," "I'm a nonsmoker," "I'm conservative." Statements like these refer to where we fit in the scheme of things. They do not clarify what makes us tick nor who we are from an internal point of view.

In fact, the true inner self is basically unpresentable in logical terms. It is a welter of contradictory emotions, behaviors, and beliefs that hides behind the "reportable" self. It can feel ten years old one day and eighty the next, while the physical, reportable self continues to be thirty-five. It can smile in the face of an appalling loss, and yet fall to pieces over a trivial setback. It can make us contemplate murdering a devoted lover and running away with a stranger. It is so riddled with ambiguities and cross-purposes that we avoid looking at it to protect our sanity. Like Perseus shunning the paralyzing face of Medusa, we can't risk more than a quick glimpse of this self in a mirror. And like Dorian Gray stashing his incriminating portrait in the attic, we dare not expose this self to the outside world.

The closest thing we have to a mirror image or portrait of our true selves is our dreams—a fact that most of us are understandably reluctant to accept. Strictly speaking, our dream content is not always hideous or humiliating. From time to time our dreams can reveal untapped reserves of beauty, compassion, and heroism in our characters. Usually, however, the self that we witness in our dreams provokes discomfort. Our specific reaction to a dream can vary from mild squeamishness at catching ourselves off guard (like the embarrassment we feel when we view ourselves on film or hear ourselves on tape) to outright revulsion against what we discover ourselves doing, or thinking, or feeling.

After analyzing over fifty thousand dreams contributed during the 1950s and 1960s by a cross-section of "normal" volunteers, Dr. Calvin Hall, an American psychologist, found that dreams perceived as "negative" outnumered dreams perceived as "positive" by four to one. Fear, including anxiety and guilt, was the most frequently cited emotional response, followed by anger and sadness. In my own discussions with dreamers, the words most commonly used to characterize dreams have been "confusing," "disturbing," "depressing," and "silly."

I believe the main reason we react this way to our dreams lies in their apparent chaos. What we observe in a typical dream is not organized for quick comprehension, nor is it compatible with our waking images of ourselves and the world we inhabit. It doesn't even add up to a satisfyingly complete story (which may be the fault of our imperfect memory of the dream, rather than of the dream itself). These unsettling aspects of the typical dream remind us of a fact that we spend a large part of our lives trying to ignore: Very little in our earthly, quotidian affairs is tidy, constant, or all-sufficient.

Behind the ever-changing roles we play, relationships we form, possessions we accumulate, and interests we pursue lies a core self concerned with the sheer process of getting through life, however uncertain it may be. This is the self we confront in our dreams. It is our essential "daimon" or dynamo and it is, by nature, uncivilized.

We recognize such a self in the biblical figure of Job, who endures even after he is stripped of everything that gives him a secure identity in the real world. We also read invocations of this self in the works of existential writers. Raskolnikov, the hero of Dostoyevsky's novel *Crime and Punishment,* for example, is inspired at one desperate point in his life to cry:

*If man were confined to a square yard of space for all eternity, surrounded by the seas in everlasting tumult and the cold air of an endless night, yet he would cling to that square yard of space, and he'd weep and exult, only to live, only to live. How vile! And how glorious!*

This core self can, indeed, be exceptionally vile or exceptionally glorious as it gropes or leaps its way through life. Two dreams I had on successive nights in October 1987 illustrate how paradoxically the dream self can behave:

**10/1:** *I am watching TV with new acquaintances at their home. I look outside a window and notice that their back yard is on fire. I don't want my acquaintances to see this and get upset, and I want to catch the end of the TV program, so I throw a sheet over their heads, run to the window, and pull down the blind. My acquaintances shake off the sheet and come to the window to see what I'm hiding. I scream and they freeze. I rush out the door clutching the sheet around me, hoping it will make me invisible.*

**10/2:** *A bus is meandering recklessly across bleak badlands with no roads. The driver appears to be simple-minded. I see this from a distance, and I long to get on the bus so that I can rescue it and so that I can get out of this desolate area. I run toward the bus making fantastically long, sure strides. Just as I'm approaching the side of the bus, it swerves and barrels directly toward me, although the driver can't see this. Instantly, I fall flat and the bus runs over me without hitting me. I spring up behind it and, grabbing the license plate, manage to pull myself onto the rear bumper. By dragging my foot as a rudder I steer the bus so that it moves safely away from this area.*

In my first dream, I react to a situation that threatens my hosts —a fire in their back yard—with outrageous denial and selfishness. Then I run out on them, hoping against all logic that I can't be seen. To my waking self, this is unacceptably childish and shameful behavior. In my second dream, however, which occurred less than twenty-four hours later, I behave admirably, exercising great courage by meeting a dangerous situation head-on. My waking self can scarcely believe such heroism.

As these contrasting dreams illustrate, the core self can be alternately stronger or weaker, nobler or more foolish than the outer, socially buttressed self. It can also be bewilderingly passive—unwilling to engage in appropriate outer-world behaviors and indifferent to what the outer-world self considers important.

The more we pay attention to the two selves and how they relate to each other, the more we will learn about our capabilities and limitations. The more we strive to integrate the two selves, the more peaceful and productive our lives will be.

## Setting Self-fulfillment Goals

The Anglo-Saxon word "hal" ("well-being") is the root of the English words "hale," "heal," "whole," and "holy." To strive for self-fulfillment is to aim for a personal state of "hal," one in which the mind and the body, the emotions and the behaviors, the inner self and the outer self function together to give health, spirit, and meaning to life.

The state of "hal" is not a state of absolute goodness, but a state of balance. We need to accept ourselves as individual human beings, and this means tolerating a certain number of mistakes, shortcoming, and failures. We must also live in an imperfect world, which means that we can never entirely escape problems, compromises, disappointments, and frustrations. What we don't have to do is victimize ourselves. If we want to lead more fulfilling lives, we can learn to overcome thoughts, feelings, and actions that are self-crippling and to cultivate those that are self-liberating.

Dreams can be an invaluable aid to self-awareness and self-development. Before turning to the inner self of your dreams, however, it's best to take a penetrating look at the self that is the audience for the dream. The following questions direct you to make that examination and to form some preliminary self-fulfillment goals:

■ **In what areas of your life (for example, individual job responsibilities, social roles, household tasks, leisure activities) are you generally competent or powerful?**

Consider each area separately and ask yourself:.Why am I this way? What feelings and behaviors do I associate with this competence or power? How do I feel and behave when this competence or power fails me?

■ **In what areas of your life are you generally incompetent or powerless?**
Consider each area separately and ask yourself: Why am I this way? What feelings and behaviors do I associate with this incompetence or powerlessness? How could I become more competent or powerful?

■ **What are some instances in your life when you have experienced great joy or excitement?**
After identifying a particular example, ask yourself: What were all the factors that contributed to that joy or excitement? What would make me experience a similar joy or excitement now? How could I change my life so that I could experience a similar joy or excitement more often?

■ **What are some instances in your life when you have experienced great fear or dread?**
After identifying a particular example, ask yourself: How did I behave at the time? Why did I behave this way? How could I have behaved more effectively? How would I handle the same situation now? How could I change my life so that it would be less subject to this kind of fear or dread?

■ **What are some instances in your life when you have experienced great anger or hostility?**
After identifying a particular example, ask yourself: How did I behave at the time? Why did I behave this way? How could I have behaved more effectively? How would I handle the same situation now? How could I change my life so that it would be less subject to this kind of anger or hostility?

■ **What are some instances in your life when you have experienced great guilt or shame?**
After identifying a particular example, ask yourself: How did I behave at the time? Why did I behave this way? How could I have behaved more effectively? How would I handle the same situation now? How could I change my life so that it would be less subject to this kind of guilt or shame?

■ **What behaviors contribute to your emotional or physical well-being?**
Consider each behavior separately and ask yourself: What motivates this behavior? How could I reinforce or enhance this type of behavior?

■ **What behaviors work to destroy your emotional or physical well-being?**
Consider each behavior separately and ask yourself: What motivates this behavior? How could I alter or eliminate this behavior so that it is less destructive?

The type of analysis you have just performed, whether you spent five minutes or five seconds with each question, is the crucial first step in any journey toward self-fulfillment. You can't expect to produce comprehensive and accurate answers during a single attempt, but you can depend upon constructive results if you use questions like these to assess your life on a regular basis. Sooner or later, self-fulfillment goals will emerge naturally from your efforts. You will convince yourself that your growth as a human being hinges on breaking a bad habit, acquiring a new skill, or making a major change in regard to your work, your home, your social arrangements, or your leisure activities.

Extending a similar kind of analysis to your dreams gives you an enormous advantage in developing and achieving self-fulfillment goals. Daily life doesn't provide enough contexts for us to recognize, much less express, all that we experience mentally, emotionally, and physically. Our dream self, however, can spontaneously create "lives" that offer such contexts. It isn't constrained by the need to be clear, rational, upbeat, consistent, or respectful of waking-life attitudes and beliefs. In dreams, we're exposed to a far broader spectrum of our actual and potential thoughts, feelings, and behaviors. We see the raw materials we bring to living, rather than the finished product we present (or think we present) in our daily life.

Dreams call us to take a sterner account of who we are. In our narrowly focused day-to-day existence, we can easily mislead ourselves. Sometimes we resort to self-deceptive strategies for the sake of expediency, particularly in the case of social or work situations. At a party, we may project a camaraderie that we don't really feel, or, during a business conference, we may instinctively suppress our enthusiasm for an idea if we sense it won't be popular. Unfortunately, self-deception can easily grow into a desperate means of survival. Whether we consciously realize it or not, we may yearn to improve our lot, but because we lack the courage or the ready means to do so, we hypnotize ourselves into believing that we can't, or that we're content the way we are. Our dream lives, by contrast, are more honest and direct. In addition to the issues that preoccupy us in our waking lives, dreams alert us to aspects of our experience that we are forgetting, denying, ignoring, overlooking, or avoiding.

In many cases, the "self-alerting" dream is full of magical occurrences. It's as if the inner self, unable to communicate what it knows or feels in real life, is forced to display this material in a bizarre, unreal dream scenario. Susan Heisland, a high school teacher in Baltimore, described such a dream during a workshop at the 1987 convention of the Association for the Study of Dreams:

*I'm late for an important daily appointment, one that gives me my "life instructions." The appointment ritual consists of going into an empty room and reading what is written on a blackboard. The room is only open for an hour and the writing is only legible for the first part of that hour.*

*Just as I fear, I am too late to read the writing clearly. All I see are some smudged letters, including one series that looks like "ylb." I watch, very frustrated, as the writing disappears completely.*

*The next thing I know, it's that night, and I am crouched outside the locked room in some bushes, spying through a crack in the wall to catch whoever it is who comes into the room to write the daily messages. Exactly at sunrise, I see my mother materialize in the locked room. She starts to write on the board. I can't make out what she's writing (it will be invisible until that special hour later on), but I'm struck speechless with how beautiful she looks and how much command she has. I feel strangely warm and inspired by the sight.*

At first, what most impressed Heisland about this dream was the supernatural apparition of her mother, who had died five years previously. "We'd never been close," Heisland admits. "I'd always disliked her; and as far as I could tell, the feeling was mutual. This dream gave me a completely different perspective."

As Heisland continued to dwell on the dream, however, her interest shifted to the blurry letters on the blackboard. This image, coupled with the frustration she felt as the letters disappeared, suggested a recurrent problem in her waking life: writer's block. During the month when she had the dream, she was struggling to compose an innovative lesson plan for the next academic year; and she was afraid she wouldn't meet the deadline. "All I'd completed was a rough syllabus—the easiest part to pull together," Heisland explains. "Then it struck me that the 'ylb' letter combination might have been referring to 'syllabus.'"

With a little more work, Heisland was not only able to draw meaningful connections between the various elements in the dream, but also able to devise a strategy aimed at resolving her waking-life dilemma. She recalled that her mother had always risen very early in the morning, long before anyone else, and that she'd resented her mother's "head start" throughout her girlhood. The dream allowed her to see what she had refused to see as a consequence of her resentment: namely, that she actually considered early rising to be a virtue and a source of power.

Despite the fact that Heisland loved to lounge in bed until the last possible moment, she was so impressed by her dream interpretation that she determined to make a ritual out of getting up at sunrise and tackling her lesson plan. She overcame her writer's block during the first early morning work session and easily met the deadline.

Not all self-alerting dreams come equipped with sci-fi plots and special effects. Even a single, realistic dream image can lead to a breakthrough in personal development, especially if the waking mind of the dreamer is prepared to receive it. Lloyd MacNair, a photojournalist in Chicago, tells this story about a dream that helped him to quit smoking:

> It happened during my third time around in the Smokenders program. I'd begun to cheat again and felt pretty hopeless about it. One night, I dreamed I was sitting in a lawn chair, about to light a cigarette. Suddenly, I smelled a whiff of chlorine. The smell was, strangely enough, so intoxicating to me that I didn't want the cigarette any longer.
>
> When I thought about this dream the next morning, I was taken back to my high school days on the swim team. At that point in my life, I hadn't started smoking yet, and the whole idea of it—the smell of it—had repelled me, as it never has since. Plus, I'd felt strong and powerful then, proud of my health and my lung capacity.
>
> After the dream, I thought about starting to swim again, to get me off smoking, but I didn't need to go that far. Just reminding myself of that dream when I had the urge for a cigarette was enough to make me stop.

MacNair is quick to point out that his chlorine dream all by itself was not a miracle-worker. One phase of Smokenders involves a similar type of aversion therapy: collecting one's cigarette butts in a jar of water and periodically sniffing them. This object lesson together with his urgent emotional need for "voice-of-God" reinforcement undoubtedly served to shape both the dream itself and his response to the dream. Nevertheless, the dream gave him the specific tool he needed to effect his self-fulfillment goal of giving up cigarettes: a touchstone, a talisman, a vivid image charged with personal meaning that offered him more hope and pleasure than his addiction.

Theoretically, MacNair could have used logic and memory to develop the same image as the one in his chlorine dream, just as Heisland could have used logic and memory to arrive at the same conclusion suggested by her blackboard dream. In practice, however, the waking lives they had created for themselves did not give them the time, space, or stimulation to think that productively. Only in their dreams were they free enough to investigate the truths of their lives. And only in their dreams could they actually realize those truths by experiencing them mentally, physically, and emotionally.

## Listening to What Dreams Say About You

Not all self-fulfillment goals are as dependent on the performance of specific tasks as the ones we've reviewed so far in this chapter (for example, communicating ideas more successfully by overcoming writer's block, or enjoying better physical health by giving up cigarette smoking). Similarly, not all dreams that assist you to fulfill your goals convey such practical help so explicitly.

Basically, our individual well-being hinges on respecting who we are and knowing what, for us, constitutes a satisfying and fruitful life. For this reason, many self-fulfillment goals are aimed at acquiring a broad self-awareness, rather than accomplishing a tightly focused self-improvement program. If we understand what kinds of work, play, and rest will make us happy, we can take a more meditative approach to dream material, and entire dreams can assume the character of visions. They can illuminate where we've been, where we are, and where we're heading.

Native Americans were (and, to a limited degree, still are) culturally conditioned to appreciate their dreams in this manner and to look to their dreams for guidance. For example, dreams gave the nineteenth-century Plains Indians their names, called them to social roles, and confirmed their unique gifts and propensities, so that they could confidently establish waking-life identities that suited themselves as well as their communities. Non–native American citizens are typically not motivated by their more secular and materialistic culture to pay special attention to their dreams; but the notion of a dream's visionary, self-fulfilling power survives in the way the word "dream" is used in the language, from Walt Disney's childlike lyric, "A Dream Is a Wish Your Heart Makes," to Martin Luther King's eloquent speech, "I Have a Dream."

The treatment of mentally, emotionally, or socially maladjusted people is the one arena in Western civilization where dreams assume "official" importance, and here the goal of self-awareness is paramount for the dreamer. Most often, the psychotherapist or mental health practitioner, in effect, helps clients make sense of their waking lives by teaching them to make sense of their dreams.

Freudian analysts rely on a process of "automatic association" to clarify the meaning of a dream. The dreamer expresses the first things that come to mind spontaneously (that is, without deliberate thought) when faced with a particular dream image, and those "unfiltered" responses are accepted as indicators of the true meaning of that image for the dreamer. Asked to respond to the image of an old upright piano in a dream, for example, the dreamer might blurt out, "pounding," "scream," and "chapel." These associations could revive the memory of a long-ago Sunday when the dreamer was severely punished for disturbing a church musicale—an emotional trauma that is unwittingly relived whenever the dreamer is disciplined.

Jungian analysts favor studying a dream as a thematic program. Individual images are translated according to archetypes that are common in the art and mythologies of numerous cultures and, therefore, that appear to be embedded in the human psyche. For example, the strong, compelling image of a circle in a dream— whether it manifests itself as the shape of a building, or the sun, or a dinner plate—may well indicate the promise, or realization, of wholeness in life, like the image of a mandala in a Buddhist scroll, or a rose window in a Gothic cathedral, or a medicine wheel in a Navaho sand painting. By examining the context of such a circular image in one of our dreams, we may gain valuable insights into what circumstances are likely to grant us harmony and balance in our waking lives.

Other professional counselors, especially those who are not trained in a particular school of dream interpretation, look for more direct clues that dreams may offer about the dreamer's identity. In 1985, Bill Thomas, a caseworker with the Los Angeles Department of Child Services, helped ten-year-old Inez Jean Sanders find herself, quite literally, through her dreams. Inez Jean was stolen from her real mother when she was five years old, and she entered the social services system after her abductor left her in a motel room a year later. Although her conscious memories of her real mother were few and fragmentary—definitely not substantial enough to enable the authorities to trace this woman—Inez remained loyal to her and fought against being adopted by foster parents. Finally, Thomas came on the scene and encouraged Inez Jean to dream about her mother. Within a year, the encouragement yielded results. Thomas told a *New York Times* reporter on February 17, 1986, "It was a dream that brought her recollections of her mother and led to the eventual reunion."

Given how hectic and perplexing life can get, most of us periodically risk losing contact with our real selves. Regular dreamwork can ensure that we maintain that contact. A formal grounding in the theories of Freud, Jung, or any other authoritative dream scholar is not necessary. Effective do-it-yourself dreamwork does not result from struggling to apply the terms of one half-understood theory to each dream, but from studying each dream on its own terms.

The interpretive process that I've found most grassroots dreamworkers use to explore "self" in their dreams is very similar to the interpretive process I outlined in Chapter Three. It consists of posing simple questions to yourself that gently lead you to consider your dream and its component parts from a variety of different angles. What feelings did the dream give you? What images and patterns occurred in the dream? What symbolic meanings can you derive from specific images and patterns in the dream? How do these feelings, images, patterns, and meanings relate to incidents in your personal history? To answer these questions, you are free to try any investigative strategy, including automatic association, the tracing of archetypal themes, and the detection of literal clues; but the signal that a particular response is on the right track is not whether it agrees with a theory, but whether it strikes you as important.

As an example of how to go about analyzing what your dreams say about your self, let me share with you another one of my personal dreamwork experiences centering on a dream I had shortly after moving from Memphis, Tennessee, to New York City. Here's the dream:

*I'm part of a large gathering of people wandering through a huge luxury apartment. It is being shown for sale to a husband and wife in the crowd. These two people seem very arrogant and jaded, but, ultimately, they indicate their desire to buy the place. I leave just as the staff is setting out an elaborate tea according to a strict schedule they follow every day. Once outside, I walk quickly to a monument—the Tomb of the Unknown Soldier. The monument consists of a line of individual soldiers from a whole series of wars. One soldier on the left-hand side stands in front of the line facing it. I leave the monument and start riding a bicycle around town with some people. Eventually we return to a house belonging to one of these people and eat some sandwiches.*

First, I considered the feelings I'd had in the dream. During the opening scene in the apartment, I'd felt aimless and dispirited, and I'd simultaneously envied and disliked the arrogant couple. I'd been anxious to leave. At the monument, I'd felt a mixture of reverence, sadness, and nostalgia. Riding the bike, I'd felt pleasure—a kind of calm, controlled excitement—and I'd enjoyed the companionship of the other bicyclists. When I first started eating sandwiches at the house, I'd felt nervous about being so intimate with people I'd just met but I soon relaxed.

Reviewing the images in the dream, I identified three different "dwellings": the apartment, the tomb, and the house. The apartment reminded me of a museum, just as the crowd reminded me of tourists. It was a place of artifice, a place where life was "stylized" and not lived. The image of the elaborate tea, which I had chosen to pass up, corroborated the impression that this was a place of manner over substance. The tomb impressed me more deeply. It recalled monuments I'd visited that had pitted my life against eternity and had forced me to take a closer look at my priorities. The house to which I'd "returned" had lacked any particular architectural distinction, but it was clearly a place where I had been capable of living a full life (being first nervous, then relaxed, and most significantly, being nourished). The pattern set up by the three different environments was reinforced by the various people I had encountered and the various ways in which I had moved along (from wandering in a crowd, to walking alone, to bicycling with others).

As for the dream's symbolic content, I was most intrigued by the monument. It had been the sharpest image in the dream, it had exhibited the greatest degree of invention (although there are many "unknown soldier" tombs in the world), and it had represented a turning point in the dream's plot—a place to which I'd deliberately walked, after finding myself in the luxury apartment and before finding myself in the house. The very concept of "the unknown soldier" that the monument had forced upon my attention seemed to apply to my own ambiguous status as a newcomer to the city: I was a soldier (I had power) but I was unknown (I lacked power). On another level, I could appreciate the tomb as an archetypal image of death and resurrection. In the dream, I had come to the tomb "quickly" after the "deadening" experience of touring the luxury apartment, and I had left the tomb riding a bicycle. Focusing strictly on the arrangement of one soldier standing in front of the others and facing them, I could see both another representation of myself (different, as any individual is, from the crowd), and an image potent enough to suggest a wide range of concepts that were appropriate to the dream, including rebellion, reflection, and return.

It was fairly easy to associate the images and apparent themes of this dream with events in my personal history. Like a great many New Yorkers, I often catch myself fantasizing about living in a spectacular apartment. The day before the dream, I had lingered over the "Luxury Homes and Estates" columns in *The New York Times Magazine*. I could also pinpoint recent occasions when I'd attended parties in dazzling apartments and when I'd been one of a large crowd of people milling through a museum (notably, during a weekend visit to the Frick Collection, which is housed on the bottom floor of a mansion). The bicycling image I could connect with my childhood, my eight years in Memphis, and even my year to date in New York, where an unused bicycle was stored along one wall of my kitchen.

My life at the time of the dream appeared quite satisfying on the surface; but underneath that surface, I could sense a vague pressure that was sapping me of energy. I knew it had something to do with "wanting more," and I automatically assumed that meant "more worldy goods." My dreamwork convinced me that this materialistic notion of what was desirable in life, however popular and appealing it might be, did not correspond to what I really wanted or needed: namely, spiritual renewal and more "nourishing" interactions with other people. The dream in conjunction with the dreamwork greatly relieved the debilitating pressure I had sensed in my life before the dream, and it has never returned with quite the same force.

---

### Experiment: Spell It Out

Select a recent dream that you've written down and analyze it, following this procedure:

1. List the major feelings you experienced in the dream. Consider each feeling separately and relate it to incidents in your waking life when you have had a strikingly similar feeling. Then look at the whole pattern of feelings in your dream and determine if there have been any incidents in your waking life that have given rise to a similar pattern of feelings. Pay special attention to recent events (starting with the previous day), but also review episodes as far back as your childhood.

2. List the major images in your dream: the settings, the characters, the behaviors, and the objects. Consider each image literally and relate it to similar images in your waking life. Then, look at the whole pattern of images and determine if there have been any specific incidents in your waking life (recent or past) that have featured a similar pattern of images.

3. Re-examine your list of images. For each image, ask yourself, "What, in general, do I associate with this image? To what other images can it be compared? What might this image be symbolizing?" Then consider the whole pattern of images and ask yourself, "What, in general, do I associate with this pattern? To what other patterns can it be compared? What might this pattern be symbolizing?"

4. Write a short paragraph describing what your dream is saying about you, based on your analysis.

## Talking to Your Dream

Because each dream that you have is a wholly original production, every single aspect of that dream says something about you. There may be a designated "you" in the dream: a character who resembles you (either now or in the past), an altogether different character whom you accept as yourself, or simply a personal perspective from which you watch the dream unfold. This "dream-you" functions most clearly as an element in the dream with which you can identify; but all the other images in the dream are also representations of you or your inner life, whatever overt references they may have to people, places, or things in the outside world.

Suppose, for example, that you dream your doctor is leading you through library stacks to his private office. You don't really want to follow him. Instead, you glance longingly out a window at the snow-capped Rocky Mountains in the distance. On one level, you can gain meaningful self-knowledge by relating the images in this dream to their realistic counterparts—visits you've made to your doctor's office, incidents in various libraries when you've felt confined, your memories or impressions of the Rocky Mountains. Maybe you'll be struck by the discovery that you are secretly afraid to get an informed opinion about your health from your doctor and that you'd prefer to be "left out in the cold," or "on vacation" from the need to worry.

The same dream, however, can resonate on an entirely different level if you view each dream image as a symbolic manifestation of some element in your interior life. This approach requires that you look beyond the "real world" identity of the image and treat it as a convenient picture that your dreaming mind borrowed for the purpose of expressing something about yourself more vividly.

To demonstrate how this kind of dream analysis works, I'll use a technique I learned from John Perkins, founder of the New York Dream Community and an expert in neurolinguistic programming. Perkins himself picked up the technique from an article written by Alissa Goldring entitled "Dreamlanguage," which appeared in the Spring 1977 edition of the *Sundance Community Dream Journal*. The technique consists mainly of adding the phrase "part-of-me" to each major image in the written dream.

Thus, the dream example I used above would be transformed into: "The doctor-part-of-me is leading me through the library-stacks-part-of-me to the private-office-part-of-me. I don't really want to go. Instead, I glance longingly out the window-part-of-me at the snow-capped-Rocky-Mountain-part-of-me."

With this reconstruction, the dream can take on an entirely new significance. It may, for example, cause you to realize that you are passively indulging your scholarly interests ("the doctor-part-of-me") and retreating within yourself ("the private-office-part-of-me"), when you actually want to change your outlook ("the window-part-of-me") and be more physically adventurous ("the snow-capped-Rocky-Mountain-part-of-me"). Your original interpretation ("I am scared to go to my doctor") remains valid; but you have also succeeded in reaching another dimension of self-awareness, using the same dream as a tool.

During his tenure in the late 1960s at the Esalen Institute in Big Sur, California, Austrian psychologist Fritz Perls popularized the concept that each dream image reflects the dreamer. As the father of gestalt therapy ("Gestalt" meaning, roughly, "whole, integrated pattern" in German), Perls devised a uniquely cathartic method of dream analysis, whereby the dreamworker conducts a spontaneous and confrontational "dialogue" with each of the images in his or her dream. The basic procedure goes like this: As the dreamer reviews the dream, he or she selects a major image and literally (i.e., vocally) asks it to explain itself. In a conversational manner, the dreamer then responds to his or her own question, taking the role of that image and literally speaking its case.

The value of Perls's gestalt dreamwork technique is that it forces the dreamer to articulate his or her immediate, "here and now" feelings about what a dream image represents. Unlike other, more reflective, procedures, it allows little room for hedging, embellishing, or intellectualizing. The dreamer as "image-impersonator" must get on with the show, and the performance can be full of surprises, coming as it does from the heart.

Several months ago, a friend of mine had the following dream:

> *A party is being held in a big nightclub to raise funds for my boss, who is running for mayor. I'm at the door collecting admissions. A long-ago girlfriend of mine appears and offers me a small Turkish coin. I'm not sure what to do.*

Intrigued by the brevity and mystery of the dream, my friend decided to investigate the major images through gestalt role-playing. Here is a partial transcript of the tape-recording he made at my request:

**Q:** (to the girlfriend): *Why have you come to this party?*
**A:** *I heard you were going to be here and I wanted to check it out. I can't believe that you're only an admissions collector and not the candidate. That's not at all like the person I remember. I wanted to see if you were okay, if something had happened to you.*
**Q:** *Why did you give me the coin?*
**A:** *I found it in my pocket, and just handed it to you because everyone else was handing you something. I don't really want to go inside.*
**Q** (to the coin): *Why are you in my dream?*
**A:** *I'm not worth anything as far as getting into this nightclub goes, but I'm very beautiful and I have great historical value. You'll want to keep me. The designs inscribed on me are far more impressive than the picture on your boss's tinny campaign buttons. Maybe I'll inspire you, so that someday there will be a coin in your honor.*

Even though my friend initially felt embarrassed about "talking to himself," he found that the gestalt method was a quick, easy, and natural way to get beyond the content of a dream to its potential meanings. Speaking of the work he did with his fund-raising dream, he remarked, "It opened up the dream for me as if I'd pressed the right spot on a Chinese puzzle-box."

Experts now tell us that the act of talking to oneself, whatever the motive, can serve an important role in self-awareness. Dr. Richard Sackett, clinical director of the Cognitive Therapy Center of New York, claims, "Some people find that actually talking aloud to themselves, as opposed to a silent dialogue, can give them a better sense of perspective." In a 1988 survey of 160 men and women twenty-two to seventy-eight years old, Dr. Paul Horton, a psychiatrist at the Child Guidance Center in Meridien, Connecticut, found that "talking to oneself" rated sixth as a source of solace and understanding ("talking with others" rated first).

Once you learn to appreciate that dreaming is, essentially, a form of talking to yourself, it's much easier to practice gestalt dreamwork without feeling self-conscious. In talking to a dream, you are simply drawing an interior dialogue into the outside world. In this sense, directly addressing a dream is analogous to praying or "vision-questing." It gives dreamwork a ceremonious quality that is appropriate to the magical nature of the dream itself.

---

### Experiment: Speak for Your Self

Choose a recent dream, one whose sensory and emotional content you can still recall fairly well. Run through the dream in your mind and determine which images you would like to clarify. Then, for each image, take turns asking and answering questions. Deliver your questions and responses out loud, in a conversational manner, relying on your imagination and good judgment to supply the "script" as you go along. Remember that you can beg an answer from *any* image in your dream, including the "dream-you," inanimate objects, and landscapes.

Here are some examples of open-ended questions to help you get started:

- Why are you in this dream?
- What do you want to show me?
- Why do you act this way?
- Why do I feel the way I do about you?
- What in my waking life made me dream of you?
- What do you want to tell me?

---

## Studying Major Themes in Your Dreams

While exploring a single dream can increase your self-awareness and put you closer to achieving your self-fulfillment goals, a much bigger reward comes from tracing a pattern through a series of dreams. The plots, settings, characters, behaviors, and objects that occur most frequently in your dreams provide the most potent clues regarding what makes you an individual. Once you isolate these dream elements and examine the way they manifest themselves in different dreams, you can reap the benefit of what they say about your ongoing life as well as what they say about the specific occasions when they reappear.

I learned a major lesson about my self through performing this kind of dreamwork early in my twenties, after a year of combining my daily-event journal with my dream journal. Rereading this journal one New Year's Day, I noticed a similarity among the following dreams:

**9/12:** *I am riding a subway with one of my students. He's totally different from me and I'm concerned about whether we'll get along on our first informal outing. Suddenly, he jerks my cap around on my head. I'm shocked by his boldness, but I also admire it. He clearly did it out of playfulness. I jerk his cap around on his head. He obviously resents this and is angry and sullen.*

**10/3:** *An attractive woman is sitting on one side of a fireplace in the lounge of a ski resort. I can see the lift running outside a picture window behind her. I sit on the other side of the fireplace, anxious to get to know her, but the fire is roaring too loudly for her to hear me calling her. To attract her attention, I do everything she does. I sit the way she does, and whenever she moves, I move the same way. Finally, she turns to her right* *to look at me, and I automatically turn to my right, away from her. I quickly look back, but she's gone.*

**11/20:** *I am vacationing with my family in a remote village in Ireland. We're staying with some relatives. I'm hurrying home alone early one evening when I suddenly realize that I'm passing between two lines of local toughs. One of them crosses his arms at shoulder level. I do the same, thinking it's a passwordlike code. Instantly, the two lines begin pelting me with stones, and I'm forced to run off.*

The main common denominator in these three dreams is my tendency to get through first-time encounters by imitating the other person—a strategy that consistently backfires. Before I noticed this behavioral trait in my dreams, I was unaware that a similar pattern existed in my waking life. A quick review of the "daily-event" entries surrounding these dreams gave me more specific information and jogged my memory. I could, indeed, recall mimicking people during awkward encounters before each dream. While the real-life characters and circumstances did not exactly match those in the dreams, there were enough points of correspondence to convince me that I was on to something.

Prodded by these cumulative insights, I could think of a number of other real-life occasions when I had reflected a new acquaintance's style or interests solely in an effort to ingratiate myself. Not all of these meetings had ended badly, but I couldn't claim that they were especially enjoyable or successful either. In the future, I made a concerted attempt to be more natural in such situations. As a result, I broke a nonproductive habit and a depressing cycle of dreams.

In many cases, we don't have to comb through a dream journal to identify a pattern in the content of our dreams. The pattern asserts itself so strongly, sometimes over years of dreaming, that we can't ignore it. Again and again we fight knife-wielding maniacs, or run from a tidal wave, or lose ourselves in a strange neighborhood. Such dreams are known as "recurring" dreams. Each separate dream in a recurring series is invariably different in some details from the other dreams, but the main images are disturbingly alike. For the sake of better self-management, let alone peace of mind, it is important to understand what these "stalling points" in our dream life represent and what triggers their repetition.

Dr. Milton Kramer, a former president of the Association for the Study of Dreams, is intent on proving just how beneficial this type of understanding can be. At the Bethesda Oak Hospital in Cincinnati, Kramer has spent the past seven years analyzing the recurring "war" dreams of Vietnam veterans who suffer from "chronic delayed post-traumatic stress syndrome." He explains the syndrome and how it operates:

> *A significant number of veterans stopped having bad nightmares after the war. Then many had recurrences after several years, often at least once a week, and sometimes nightly. Dreams are very reactive to immediate events. When these vets face trauma in their current lives, usually divorce, it stimulates rage left over from the war. The syndrome is representative of their current life's happenings, an interweaving of the present and the past.*

Working on their dreams with Kramer has helped many of these veterans learn to cope more effectively with the stress in their waking lives; and, consequently, their "war" dreams have recurred with far less frequency. While the syndrome itself may never disappear completely, the fear and despair associated with the syndrome have been significantly reduced.

Recurring dreams or dream elements are not always negative. We can be pleasantly surprised and invigorated by a return visit to a favorite dream landscape or a repeat encounter with a beloved dream character, and it is just as fruitful to study these recurring positive images as it is to study the negative ones. If nothing else, they can tell us a great deal about what truly gives us pleasure in life.

A friend of mine repeatedly dreams of a strange, golden-haired young man who takes her on adventures. For a long time, she thought of it as an erotic image, summoned by sexual longings in her waking life. When she began charting these dreams in her journal, however, she realized that the golden-haired boy served as much more than just a dream lover. He tended to appear in her dreams as a symbol of confirmation whenever she did something constructive in her waking life or whenever she made a decision that turned out to be the right one.

It is also especially worthwhile to trace the recurring identities that we give ourselves in dreams—identities that are not necessarily positive or negative in themselves but can be either exciting or scary from the point of view of our waking-life identities. In their dreams, males may appear as females; heterosexuals, as homosexuals; libertines, as priests; milquetoasts, as murderers; teenagers, as senior citizens. Gaining a deeper appreciation of the recurring identities that you assume in your dreams can only assist your efforts to integrate the different aspects of your personality, so that you can attain the "wholeness" that is inseparable from self-fulfillment.

Every few months in my own dream life, I appear as a bearded man living a primitive life in a forest with a young daughter, roughly four to six years old. I'm not sure precisely what this dream-image represents. I'm inclined to believe it is a composite image developed from different intriguing life possibilities that I was denied, or that I rejected, or that I imagined for myself as I grew up: what Liam Hudson, a professor of psychology at England's Brunel University, calls "alternative repertoires of identity and need." Hudson refers to these repertoires in his book *Night Life* as "residual paths" that our lives did not take, due to accidents of birth, cultural forces, or our own life choices. He adds:

*These residual paths may well be ones that the individual in question is half willing to entertain in the form of sexual reveries or fantasies, or in his choice of jokes; or to acknowledge more obliquely in the form of idiosyncracies of taste or social mannerism that are subtly out of keeping with the path to which he is explicitly committed. They nonetheless remain in the margin of his way of life as it is explicitly constituted, and as such are precisely the kind of material on which, when dreaming, his imagination will tend to feed. (from Liam Hudson,* Night Life, New York: St. Martin's Press, 1986, p. 125)

Whatever lies behind the "bearded-man-with-daughter" identity that I experience in my dream life, I derive definite value from attending to it. At critical times in my life, it prompts me to reaffirm my love of the outdoors and my love of children (which risk going unacknowledged in my waking life, since I don't have children of my own and I live in an urban environment). More than this, it educates me about what it feels like to be responsible for my own survival and for the successful maturation of a loved one. In short, it's a point of self-reference that tells me a little bit more about who I am and what may be involved, for good and ill, in pursuing the self-fulfillment goals I set for myself.

---

## Experiment: Take Stock of Your Dreams

Periodically conduct an inventory of the dreams you've collected by following this procedure:

1. On a blank sheet of paper, create six vertical columns with these headings: (1) date and title, (2) characters, (3) settings, (4) objects, (5) behaviors, and (6) feelings.

2. For each dream, list individual items in the appropriate columns. When you are finished with a dream, draw a bold horizontal line across the page to separate these responses from the ones that pertain to the next dream.

3. After you've worked through a manageable number of dreams (ten dreams is a good minimum base for a single

---

session, but you may have the time and patience to handle many more), look at each column separately and take note of repeated items. For each repeated item, ask yourself, "How does this item relate to my waking life (present and/or past)? What might account for its recurrence?"

4. When you have finished looking at individual items, compare whole dreams that have two or more points of similarity (for example, the same character and the same setting, or the same object and the same feeling). For each comparison, ask yourself, "How do these dreams as a group relate to any pattern in my waking life (present and/or past)? What might account for the recurrence of this type of dream? What possible meaning can I derive from the differences among these otherwise similar dreams?"

## The Self and Dreams: Substance and Shadow

Dreams do not tell us what is right or wrong with our waking lives. Only the conscious mind can make such judgments. Instead, dreams give us a shifting perspective on the conflicts that our waking self experiences—conflicts that the conscious mind may not even recognize or be able to frame as issues requiring judgment.

In our dreams we are free to explore our wishes and fears, free to admit our prejudices and animosities, and free to forgive our mistakes and deficiences. We can liberate our vision of who we are and who we can become not only from the expectations of those around us, but also from our own waking-life expectations. We cease to be held back by the "solid" verities of the real world.

Whatever specific advice we may extract from dreams, their major contribution to our self-fulfillment is that they keep us from becoming rutted in our day-to-day roles. They continually remind us that, as human beings, we are ever-developing processes rather than static personalities.

While our dream life may often seem bizarre and ephemeral when we're awake, we must remind ourselves that our waking life often seems monotonous and brutish in our dreams. Both points of view need to be honored for what they can teach us. William Butler Yeats, keenly aware of this need, offers a haunting plea for the dream perspective in his poem "The Shadowy Waters":

> *All would be well*
> *Could we but give us wholly to the dreams,*
> *And get into their world that to the sense*
> *Is shadow, and not linger wretchedly*
> *Among substantial things; for it is dreams*
> *That lift us to the flowing, changing world*
> *That the heart longs for.*

# 5

# Dreams and Relationships

**Pamela Ewing:** *It was awful. It was a nightmare. It was terrible . . . I felt like it was all so real.*
**Bobby Ewing:** *Pam, it's over. None of that happened.*

On September 26, 1986, an estimated 50 million Americans tuned in to the season premiere of *Dallas*. They were eager to find out how writers for the top-ranked CBS television series were going to explain the return of Bobby Ewing, a beloved character who had died on-screen, hooked to a heartbeat monitor, sixteen months earlier. With the dialogue quoted above, twenty-two previous episodes of *Dallas* were dismissed as the dream of his wife, Pamela; and one hundred million viewing eyes barely blinked.

Most experts claim that it is impossible to dream so much material in a single evening. (In repeated experiments, doctors have clocked a sleeping subject's dream time by monitoring rapid eye movements; then, after waking the subject the instant a dream has ended, they've clocked the time it has taken the subject to re-enact his or her dream. The two time periods have always proved to be virtually the same.) Technicalities aside, however, it's easy to understand why the general public was willing to accept that over a year of *Dallas* had been a dream. The major plot fare of soap operas — human relationships — is also the major plot fare of dreams. Both media excel at dramatizing all the potential story lines among a given set of characters. Best friends betray each other. Mortal enemies discover they are brothers. Dead lovers reappear to challenge new ones.

As the poet Adrienne Rich wrote, "The possibilities that exist between two people, or among a group of people, are a kind of alchemy. They are the most interesting things in life." In fact, we can't resist playing with such possibilities. The continuing television soap opera, a notoriously addictive programming format, offers evidence that this obsession exists on a communal level; our dreams shows us that it also exists on a private level.

The human being is a social animal. Because we derive a major part of our own self-images from our interactions with others, it's no wonder that we so frequently test our relationships in our dreams. What would I be like if my mate grew bored with me? If my mother were there to watch me kick up my heels at a party? If my boss became my slave for a day? If my child were kidnapped? There are enough mysteries and sources of conflict in any relationship to allow plenty of scope for the imagination.

When we dream of people who are important to us, we may be exploring issues that are too upsetting to think about on a conscious level: for example, intimacy taboos that separate us, half truths that bind us together, ambivalences that keep us from being totally comfortable with each other. Such controversial material makes for memorable dream drama, which probably explains why so many of the contributions to the *Dream Network Bulletin* during the time I was an editor dealt with these kinds of dreams. Here's part of a 1984 letter from a male graduate student at Michigan State University:

*During the past spring, I had a number of dreams in which I struck my sister in anger over some trivial event. In the dreams, she would either hit me back or just turn around and leave. I've never struck my sister, or even thought about doing it, so those dreams shook me up pretty badly. In a couple of dreams, there were erotic overtones to the violence, as if I were wrestling with her, and these dreams were really disturbing.*

*One day I ran into a friend of mine from home who also goes to Michigan State, and he said that he and my sister had had coffee together over the spring break. Immediately, I recalled those dreams and I understood them. I missed not being the main man in her life anymore; and in my dreams, I was acting out the anger and frustration I felt. I wouldn't have realized what was going on if my dreams hadn't brought it to my attention.*

When we dream of people who used to be important to us but no longer are, we may be trying to resolve unfinished business or to start new business altogether. Classmates of mine from grade school occasionally pop up in my dreams, as do former girlfriends, roommates, colleagues, and employers. Almost always I can identify an unsettling emotion or experience that I associate with the person in question — some area that is still "raw" in my memory.

In junior high, for example, I once totally alienated a girl by teasing her about wearing thick glasses. Three years later, I was passionately attracted to her, but that awkward incident in our history kept us from getting together. Now, every so often, she shows up in one of my dreams. Sometimes I can pinpoint a reason for her appearance (I might have met someone that day who resembled her); sometimes I can't. Whatever the case, her appearance always reminds me to be aware of the negative effect that teasing someone can have.

The more I discuss such visitations with other dreamers, the more I believe that our dreams may be holding us accountable for our pasts, or (to bend a Buddhist concept) that we may be working out our karma in our dreams. The basic premise of this theory is simple and supremely just: If we don't follow through on the consequences of our thoughts, words, and deeds in our waking lives, we may wind up doing so in our dream lives. We may think we have gotten away with thoughtlessness to others, but our dreams may not let us off the hook. We may no longer demand justice from someone who did us wrong, but our dreams may keep the case alive. We may have broken our vows to a high school sweetheart, but our dreams may be pledged to that person forever.

When we dream of virtual strangers, we can exhibit aspects of ourselves that we conceal from our closer associates. We can be stronger, weaker, more inhibited, less inhibited, better, or worse than we feel obliged to be among the people who see us on a regular basis. If the stranger is considerably different from us or the individuals to whom we relate in our waking lives, then the effect is intensified.

A woman in my dreamwork group (whom I'll call "Jill") has recorded many dreams that exemplify this pattern. Jill once dreamed about a secretary she'd encountered the week before during a one-time visit to a prospective client. In her dream, the secretary spoke with a more condescending manner and a thicker Oxford-English accent than she had displayed in real life, and Jill detested her for it. Jill raged until she foamed at the mouth, and finally, she swept all the paperwork off the secretary's desk.

In reviewing the dream, Jill could accept that her waking-life visit as a whole had been far more discouraging than her conscious mind had acknowledged it to be. The dream had brought her frustration to the surface in the form of overt hostility, and the secretary (who, in reality, had barely spoken to her) had served as an appropriately "unknown" target—although Jill admitted that her choice of opponent might have been influenced by a latent prejudice against the British.

Another dream Jill shared with the group featured a complete stranger in a role that contrasted sharply with the role of the secretary in the dream I just recounted. Jill, who is white, dreamed she was sitting in an airport lounge next to a black man. The public address system kept sputtering unintelligible announcements, and

Jill and the black man found themselves laughing at the same moments. Eventually, she realized that she wanted to go out with the man, so she turned on all her charm, chatting with him and flirting with him until she woke up. Jill told the group that she was seldom so forthcoming in real life and had never dated a black man. Her dream exchange with a different kind of man, in her opinion, enabled her inner self to try out a different kind of behavior.

We can't help being curious about dreams that depict us interacting with others in unusual ways. Like soap operas, they seem deliberately designed to shock, tantalize, or mystify. Far more common, however, and equally instructive, are dreams that focus on the *actual* quality of our *present* relationships. With very little thought, we can tell when one of our dreams falls into this latter category instead of the former one. We instinctively recognize that the dream is conveying what is really happening—whether we consciously know it or not—in our waking-life experience with another individual.

In a composition course I taught at Memphis State University, I asked students to keep a journal of incidents in their lives that had the potential to be developed into essays or short stories. One married student named Connie made the following entry in her journal:

> Last night I dreamed that I saw a jade plant and a corn plant growing out of the same pot in our living room. I knew they were too close and I had to pull them apart and replant them in separate pots, but I didn't know how to do this without killing them both. Jim (my husband) came into the room and saw that I was worried about something. I thought he'd be upset that I was so worked up about a plant, so I didn't say anything. Then I saw him looking at the plant, so I told him what I thought needed to be done. He said he knew how to do it and they would both live, no problem.
>
> When I woke up . . . I knew the dream had been about my fears that Jim and I were growing too dependent on each other and were living too close together. For one thing, we're both in school; we spend our free time

*together; and when we study, our desks are both in the living room. . . .
The dream made me feel more confident about discussing this problem
with Jim.*

Connie's dream did not include any exotic behavior or images to
divert her attention from her daily preoccupations. What it did was
provide succinct commentary on a vague, real-life problem that had
been perplexing her for several months. When we talked about the
dream later, I pointed out that the words "jade" and "corn" might
have been referring to the names "James" and "Connie," since they
possess similar sounds; but Connie didn't need to look for such
clues to derive meaning from the dream. The dream was confirm-
ing a situation to which she was already consciously attuned. In her
waking life, she had not been able to go beyond her anxiety about
this situation. Her dream took her beyond that anxiety to a more
positive and optimistic readiness to work the problem out.

Some dreams about people we know in waking life are so in-
sightful that they seem almost clairvoyant. Possibly they are. It's
also possible, however, that they are inspired by a series of waking-
life observations that failed to make any significant impression on
the conscious mind, but that the dreaming mind tracked and as-
sembled into a dream portrait. Ann Faraday recounts such a dream
in *Dream Power,* her seminal book on experiential dreamwork:

*I once dreamed that I opened the morning paper at breakfast and saw a
large photograph of a rather humorless psychoanalyst friend of mine. He
stood smiling broadly between the figures of Frank Sinatra and Tony
Curtis, and the caption below read in large letters "The Singing Psychiatrist." The newspaper said he had been chosen from hundreds of appli-
cants to play the romantic lead in a new musical film with the two famous
stars.*

Faraday was unable to reconcile this dream with her waking-life
perception of her friend, mainly because he presented himself as a
strict academician who had serious reservations about Faraday's

popularization of psychological topics in the press and on television. When she checked to see if there was some objective truth in the dream vision, she discovered that her friend had recently advertised in the press for his own new program of encounter and sensitivity-training groups — a development completely at odds with the beliefs he'd always expressed to Faraday. While he was not becoming a movie star, he was indeed following in Faraday's footsteps by becoming a media "star." In her discussion of the dream, Faraday remarks:

> Looking back, I was able to see that he had quizzed me about groups, books, and all relevant information on the subject to a degree which was quite out of keeping with his apparent disinterest. I had obviously registered this discrepancy at the back of my mind and my dream had thrown up a story around the subliminal suspicion that he was encroaching on my territory. (from Ann Faraday, Dream Power, New York: Berkley Books, 1973, pp. 169–171)

In many cases, dreams give us a point of view on a person we know that may not be not objectively or literally accurate, but nevertheless helps us to interact with that person more effectively in our waking lives. A friend of mine who does a lot of ghostwriting once collaborated with a psychiatrist on a book based on the psychiatrist's practice. The psychiatrist persisted in accusing my friend of being a "moralistic Catholic" who did not possess the psychiatrist's cool, professional detachment when it came to putting together case histories of individual patients. "I gave all that stuff up," the psychiatrist would say, referring to his own Catholic past. These attacks were not meant as serious criticisms. My friend is not a practicing Catholic or a moralist, and the collaborator knew this. The attacks were simply part of a "you versus me" dialogue that was getting on my friend's nerves.

One night, during a period when my friend was sorely troubled by this misguided teasing, he dreamed he was serving Mass for a priest who was wearing a mask. At the end of the Mass, the priest took off his mask and revealed himself to be the psychiatrist.

When we discussed the dream several weeks later, my friend told me:

> At first I was shocked when I saw that the priest was G___ [his collabo-
> rator]. Then I felt vindicated, thinking that G___ himself might be a
> Catholic-behind-a-mask. Finally, I figured out that the dream was talking
> about our working relationship, not the possibility that G___ was a closet
> Catholic. As my dreaming mind saw it, G___ was setting himself up as a
> "counter-priest" or authority figure, and I was being cast as someone who
> would submissively "serve" him. It made me consider the fact that he was
> uncomfortable having to rely on me for writing expertise. I began to think
> of his running joke as a mask——a clumsy means of discussing what to
> him was an awkward relationship——and it made me much better able to
> deal with him.

Our rational minds can only *tell* us that the myths, fantasies, and illusions operating in our relationships have as much potential power, for good or for bad, as the so-called realities have. Our dreams can *convince* us—through giving us new perspectives—that it's true.

## Setting Goals for Relationships

Most self-help books over the past generation have taken a one-sided approach to setting goals for relationships. The bottom line tends to be "What's in it for me?" We're told that our proper mission in society is to win friends, influence strangers, attract lovers, and assert our rights with everyone we encounter. And we're trained to formulate objectives that are basically egocentric: Make X more interested in me, stop Y from bothering me, get Z to take over some of my workload, convince X, Y, and Z to see things my way.

There's nothing intrinsically wrong with such objectives; but they're so "me"-oriented that they risk being shortsighted and, therefore, unattainable, inappropriate, or even undesirable once they're applied to a specific interpersonal situation. We might change our minds about the types of relationships we want with other people if we first take some time to develop a deeper appreciation of their needs, capabilities, and desires. Given this possibility, the egoist's motto should rightly be the same as the altruist's motto: "Unless I look beyond myself to determine what is best for all parties, I won't be able to appreciate what is best in the long run for me."

Any relationship, no matter how tenuous, represents more than a simple sum of interactions between two people. At some level, it's a merger of identities. The mere fact that someone else has entered our conscious world means that he or she, from then on, is an indissoluble part of our life history, with a potential or actual impact on our thoughts, deeds, and dreams that defies estimation. Multiparty relationships, such as families or work teams, represent mergings of multiple identities. By extension, our individual personalities are merged with the human collective—the race itself.

We need to be mindful of these facts when we contemplate our relationships. Whatever we do in regard to another person also affects ourselves and a whole complex of individuals whose lives are inextricably bound together. For this reason, the goals we form for our relationships must be cooperative ones, that is, they must allow some room for all relevant parties to participate as they see fit. Before we can determine what these goals should be, we need to consider how our individual relationships already work, from each party's perspective as well as from the perspective of a detached observer. Then we need to imagine how they might work, given various hypothetical changes.

Our dreams shed a uniquely revealing light on the inner character of our relationships, and that light works, as light-of-day thinking can't, to illuminate some of the healthy and unhealthy ways in which we are, or could be, merged with others. Your personal dream information, together with the information you acquire from answering the following questions, can help you form goals for your relationships that are achievable, productive, and responsible.

Consider all your waking-life relationships as a whole and ask yourself these questions:

- **What kinds of relationships in my life have been the most successful or satisfying for both parties?**

- **What kinds of relationships have been the least successful or satisfying for both parties?**

- **What kinds of relationships would I like to have that I haven't had before or don't have now?**

- **What aspects of my life (skills, knowledge, possessions, activities, thoughts, memories, emotions) have I repeatedly shared with others?**

- **What aspects of my life have I usually not shared with others?**

- **What aspects of my life could I conceivably share with others that I haven't shared so far?**

- **What aspects of my life would I most like to share with others, given the chance?**

- **Do patterns exist among my relationships?**
  Consider, for example:
  - the types of friends you make
  - the types of associates with whom you work
  - the types of people with whom you fall in love
  - the way your friendships, associations, and love affairs begin, progress, and conclude
  - what other people expect from you

- what you expect from other people
- the praises and criticisms that other people bestow upon you
- the praises and criticisms you bestow upon other people

**■ What changes would I like to make in these patterns?**

Consider each pattern separately, and ask yourself what you could do to make those changes and what other people could do to help you make those changes.

Now, consider each of your important current relationships individually and ask yourself:

**■ What are the positive aspects of this relationship? How did they develop? How might they be strengthened?**

**■ What are the negative aspects of this relationship? How did they develop? How might they be overcome?**

**■ What do I need from X (the other person)? How could I get it?**

**■ What does X need from me? How could I give it to X?**

**■ What don't I understand about X and/or our relationship? How might I learn to understand X and/or our relationship better?**

Questions like these compel us to relive our relationships as they were, as they might have been, and as they could be. They also force us to swap roles in our relationships and go through the same process of reliving them. Our dreams do all this and more.

Most significantly, dreams project feelings, insights, and possibilities pertaining to our relationships that our conscious minds can't rationally articulate or act upon. One of the members of my dream group volunteered this illustration:

> *For years, I remained friends with an ex-colleague who was becoming more and more of a social climber. Finally, I'd had it with his name-dropping, so I allowed us to drift apart by not returning his calls or phoning him. I felt guilty for doing this, but every time I thought about calling him, I talked myself out of it. It was a real impasse, and I knew part of the problem was that, to some extent, I envied him his social connections.*
>
> *Then, out of the blue, I had a dream in which I saw this guy fall on some sharp rocks and hurt himself. I found myself enormously concerned for his welfare. I remember looking down onto the top of his head below me as I pulled him up and feeling very compassionate toward him. The dream showed me that, yeah, if anything bad happened to him, I'd be upset; in other words, that I cared about him and that I'd feel better if I were in a position to help him out. Knowing this, I didn't have any problem renewing the friendship. So much for my guilt, and amazingly, he doesn't seem to get on my nerves as much anymore.*

Dreams can also give us a degree of detachment from our "me" point of view that our waking life just can't offer. Marty Bollach, a congressional staffer and a member of the Metro DC Dream Community, told me about a dream that performed this important service for her when she was a senior in college:

> *The dream started out with a young man and a young woman inside an ancient temple, standing before two gigantic living statues, like Egyptian gods. I was an observer in the background. The whole atmosphere was highly charged with romance and grandeur. One of the statues said to the couple, "Thou shalt be together forever," and the young woman gave what seemed to be almost a ceremonial sigh of pleasure.*
>
> *Right after this I noticed that the young man's head was turning toward a strip of light around a nearby exit, and instantly I became the*

*young woman. I walked past that young man and out that exit. I was on a lively, colorful city street, and I knew that the temple I had left was a phony stage set. I felt much more invigorated being on the street among all those bustling people.*

Bollach had no trouble recognizing the young man and the young woman as herself and her boyfriend. Although they thought of themselves as a model couple and were facing the prospect of marriage after graduation, Bollach suspected that her boyfriend was a bit restless. This scared her, until the dream allowed her to entertain the notion that she, too, might enjoy more freedom. "The statues struck me right away as stagey, larger-than-life self-images that held us in thrall," Bollach noted, "but the truly exciting part of the dream was that I became a background observer, saw myself and the scene I was in, and then repossessed myself and took action: I walked away from a dead situation toward the light."

## Matching Dreams with Waking-Life Relationships

In many instances, the "facts" in a dream relationship are easily referrable to the facts in a waking-life relationship. As in Bollach's Egyptian temple dream, the dream characters, their activities, and the context in which they find themselves all point to a specific real-world situation, and the dreamer has no doubt about the connection. Often, the situation is one that has already provoked so much conscious speculation that the dreamer is instantly familiar with the tone of the dream as it unfolds and, when analyzing the dream later, can establish correspondences to that situation for virtually all of the details in the dream.

Even when the source material of a dream relationship seems obvious, however, it's important to remember that the person to whom we relate in a dream is a character we have created in someone else's image. The character bears comparison to his or her real-life counterpart but is not identical to that counterpart. Out of fear, pain, rage, or sheer perversity, we can draw vicious portraits of essentially innocent, well-meaning people; and out of hope, gratitude, love, or sheer elation, we can idealize people who are, in fact, abusive to us.

The truth of a dream must always be tested against objective reality. In doing so, we may find that a dream character inspires genuine revelations about that character's real-life equivalent. On the other hand, we may find, as Marty Bollach did, that we have created a dream character with a real-life equivalent primarily in order to spark a revelation about ourselves.

When the real-life source material of a dream relationship is *not* obvious to us, we have to proceed with even greater care. It's quite common to dream about someone we know in a strange, new context or behaving in a way that doesn't fit with his or her waking-life patterns. Many times, a little poetic imagination will solve the puzzle. For example, suppose a man dreams that his grandmother flirts with him and asks him for a date. He may get very perplexed, worried, and even appalled about the incestuous overtones of this dream; but, in fact, the reason he produced this dream image may be much more innocent. The image may have resulted from a recent conversation he had with his grandmother that brought back memories of a childhood outing with her—an outing that was special to him then in some of the ways that a date is special to him now.

If you are struck by the inappropriateness of a dream character's behavior to his or her real-life counterpart and no satisfactory explanation comes to mind, the answer could well be that the character in your dream does not represent his or her real-life equivalent at all. Instead, the character may represent some aspect of you: a quality that both you and the real-life equivalent possess, a trait that the real-life equivalent brings out in you, or a role that you commonly play with the real-life equivalent. The dream character could just be a dummy figure that you place in your dream in order to express yourself more dynamically. You may choose to fight your daughter in a dream, for example, because you yourself behaved in a childish way during the day; or you may wish to have a good, long talk with yourself in your waking life, so you dream of the last person with whom you had a good, long talk.

It's also possible that the dream character is not who he or she appears to be but a substitute for another person in your waking life. Usually, such a substitution makes a telling point regarding some similarity between the two individuals involved. You may dream, for example, that your normally mild-mannered spouse is ordering you around with the same brusqueness that your boss typically displays. The dream may not mean anything to you as a portrait of your spouse, but it may mean a great deal if you substitute "boss" for "spouse." It may lead you to recognize that your relationship with your boss is taking on some of the aspects of your relationship with your spouse. Perhaps you're becoming more emotionally attached to your boss, or maybe you're starting to interact with your boss in some of the ways you interact with your spouse. These developments in your relationship may be positive or negative. Possibly your dream can help you decide. Whatever the case, your dream is calling attention to a situation that your waking mind is not consciously addressing.

Frequently the dreaming mind simply borrows a familiar face from your waking life to use as a symbol. Your next-door neighbor, a trumpet player, may show up in a dream as your companion in a nightclub. His appearance may have nothing to do with your relationship as neighbors or even as observers of each other. Instead, the music in the dream may have prompted you to cast your neighbor—the only musician you know personally—as someone appropriate for this environment. You may be baffled about a dream in which you shove one of your colleagues out your office window, until you try looking at the colleague as a symbol of all the people with whom you work.

I'm especially fascinated by the appearance of celebrities in dreams. Although they often function in dreams as clear substitutes for people we know who resemble them or the roles they perform,

I believe that celebrities also resonate in dreams as symbols of larger issues. Like the ancient Greek and Roman gods and goddesses, the celebrities who appear in a given person's dreams may individually represent certain qualities, values, and attributes that preoccupy that person, because of either who that person is, the life that person leads, or the culture in which that person lives. The increasingly secular nature of present-day society, combined with a general lack of real-life heroes, could certainly contribute to such a phenomenon.

For years, Dee Burton, a New York therapist, noticed a tendency among many of her patients to dream of Woody Allen, a fact of special interest to her because she, too, had dreams of Woody Allen. In 1984, she advertised for volunteers with similar experiences and was inundated with calls and letters from all fifty states, Canada, the United Kingdom, Japan, Italy, West Germany, Austria, and Belgium. "Woody Allen," she concluded, "may well appear in the dreams of millions." Her subsequent book, *I Dream of Woody* (Morrow, 1984), reprints a mere eighty of the responses.

In discussing these dreams, Burton claims that Woody Allen has, in a way, entered the collective unconscious as a symbol of the death-haunted underdog who triumphs because of his wit and artistic integrity. "More than anything else," declares Burton, "Woody Allen stands for a search for sanity in a shallow world."

Putting aside the "Woody Allen" dream craze and Burton's interesting (if somewhat grandiose) claims, most celebrity dreams do seem to convey symbolic messages relating to the culture in which we live; but they also have a very personal dimension. During the last year, I have dreamed of a number of celebrities, including Kathleen Turner, Ed Koch, Lech Walesa, Diane Sawyer, Mike Tyson, Harrison Ford, and the Duchess of York. In some dreams, the celebrity was a fantasy friend, lover, or antagonist: a partner in a relationship that my dreaming mind imagined as some sort of ideal of its type. In other cases, I know I dreamed of a particular celebrity because I did, in a sense, have a relationship with him or her in my waking life. I repeatedly saw films and pictures of the celebrity and occasionally thought about the celebrity. My dream was just supplying the missing half—the celebrity's actually responding to me. The dream was fulfilling a wish, and it was allowing me to explore the dynamics of a hypothetical relationship.

As I've already mentioned, dreams in which we have a relationship with someone we don't recognize can give us the opportunity to try out different interactive behaviors; but before we write off these dream characters as strangers, we need to make sure they aren't people we know in disguise. Many times a strange dream character is a composite of several people in our waking life. The mysterious dream lover of one woman whom I met at a dream-study workshop turned out on closer examination to have the hair of one former lover, the body shape of another, and the mannerisms of her father—a character capable of communicating a great deal to her about specific men in her life as well as about the general type of man to whom she is likely to be attracted.

Finally, we should be mindful that a dream can present a person we know from our waking life as an animal or a thing, rather than a human character. Psychologist Gayle Delaney, currently a consultant at the San Francisco Dream Center, discussed dreams of this nature on syndicated television's *Oprah Winfrey Show* (April 22, 1987). One of Delaney's clients dreamed that she wanted to get rid of a rat that was hanging around her bedroom. A little dreamwork convinced her that the rat represented her lover. Another client dreamed that an unseen assailant who was chasing her with a knife suddenly turned into a puddle. She tasted the puddle and it was the same brand of cognac that her father, a belligerent alcoholic, drank.

A member of my dreamwork group once dreamed that a red and white windmill stood in front of his boss's office door, keeping him from getting inside. Days later, he noticed that one of his coworkers was wearing a red and white dress with a criss-cross pattern similar to the arms of a windmill. It was a dress she often wore and, sure enough, she was a rival who consistently "stood in his way" when he tried to make an impression on his boss.

Determining who's who (or what's who) in your dreams is not as tricky in practice as it may seem from some of the examples we've reviewed. Your gut feeling is your best guide. Given proper consideration, it will signal to you when there's more to a dream character or a dream relationship than is immediately apparent.

Another excellent and entertaining way to understand how the characters and images in your dreams may be commenting on your real-life relationships is to subject those dream characters and images to a systematic analysis. It's not as if you are searching for the "right" interpretation. There may be many interpretations that are equally "right." What you are seeking is a reading that makes the dream click for you; in other words, a reading that allows the dream to reveal to you something significant about one (or more) of your waking-life relationships.

## Experiment: Dream Dragnet

The next time you have a puzzling dream encounter with a seemingly familiar character, or a stranger, or an animal, or even a thing, do what a police investigator would do: Suspect everyone, assemble the evidence into exhibits, conduct a line-up, and accuse no one without establishing reasonable cause. To perform your investigation, follow these three steps:

1. Write a "police blotter" description of the dream character that isolates his or her individual characteristics. Include name (if expressed in the dream), sex, race, age, height, weight, complexion, hair color and style, facial expressions, distinguishing marks, mannerisms, clothing. If the target of your investigation is an animal or an object, list its dominant qualities. Then review your description and list or consider the people in your life who have several of those same characteristics or qualities.

2. Write a "clue board" that isolates the various images and events in the dream that can be associated with the dream character, animal, or object. Include places where he or she

was seen, his or her actions and reactions, the actions and reactions of other characters toward him or her, objects with which he or she came in contact. (If the target of your investigation is an animal or an object, you may want to personify it in your imagination in order to make this task easier and more revealing.) After you've finished, review the items on your clue board. Then consider the people in your life whom you can associate with images or events that are similar to those on your board.

3. Compare the review sheet for your police blotter and the review sheet for your clue board. If several items on each sheet suggest the same specific individual in your life, think about your relationship with that individual. Use your imagination to establish possible motives for his or her behavior in your dream.

## Determining What Action to Take

It's the stuff of cartoons and comedies. A husband dreams that his wife scolds him, so he's mean to her at breakfast. A secretary dreams that her boss makes love to her, so she's shy with him at the office. A child dreams that her baby brother runs away, so she won't let him out of her sight for the rest of the week. As a fact of life, however, involuntary dream-inspired behavior is not always a laughing matter.

A 1983 study by Dr. Milton Kramer and Dr. Thomas Roth at the Veterans Hospital in Cincinnati indicated that dreams are very likely to influence our mood in the morning, with frustrating dreams causing a testy mood and nice dreams making us happy. When we put this information together with Dr. Calvin Hall's conclusion that two-thirds of our dreams are unpleasant, we have a possible explanation for why so many people seem to be grumpy during the first couple of hours after waking. We're also presented with a challenge: What, if anything, should be our response to a disturbing dream about one of our relationships?

A good general procedure is to record the dream as soon as possible and then devote some time to working with it, even if it's only a few minutes. This quick review serves several purposes. It gives you an immediate and highly appropriate outlet for your feelings. It also forces you to assume responsibility for the dream (which is, after all, *your* imaginative creation) before you unknowingly foist that responsibility on someone else. And it ensures that you'll remember the dream, in case the dream is communicating truths about the relationship that your conscious mind has not yet processed.

Many dreams about relationships will offer their own built-in advice, and if this advice is constructive in general and appeals to you, it's worth trying out, particularly if it has the potential to turn a bad situation into a better one. A member of the Brooklyn Dream Community told me the following dream he had about his upstairs neighbors—a Santo Domingan family with which he frequently quarrels:

> *I notice that water is dripping into my bathroom from the F___s' bathroom, so I start shouting at them. I get no answer, so I go upstairs and I see three or four illegal aliens there. They don't see me and my voice won't come to shout. I return to my apartment and Nana (my grandmother, who died a year ago) is there, mopping up the floor. She has a heavenly smile and tells me that the secret of the problem is to help.*

The dream seemed to be saying to this dreamer, in an especially ethereal way, that he and the F___s and even illegal aliens (whom he had perhaps unconsciously associated with the F___s) "shared the same water" and that he should be compassionate rather than confrontational. He decided to follow this advice by extending small courtesies to the F___s and offering to work with the F___s on issues that would lead to a better living situation for both households. As a result, the incidence of trouble and friction between the two neighbors has decreased dramatically.

Sometimes the tips we get in dreams are very subtle ones. For months, a friend of mine who's an editor for a New York publishing firm was having difficulties working with one of her colleagues. One night she dreamed that she was sitting *beside* the colleague instead of *across* from her, her usual position. They got along so well together in this dream that she tried out the new seating arrangement at the office.

"Sitting next to her definitely improved our rapport," she told me, "and I have no idea why. It could be that my whole attitude was different after the dream, or that people tend to work better sitting next to each other, but I don't think either reason wholly accounts for it. Subconsciously I just sensed that for the two of us, this way of sitting would be better."

---

### Experiment: Take It from a Dream

The next time you have a dream that you can connect with a specific person in your life, study the dream closely to determine whether you can learn anything from it that might enhance your relationship with this individual. Here is a process for conducting this study:

1. Consider the dream on its own terms and ask yourself these questions:
   - How do the other person and I first come together in the dream?
   - How does the other person behave in the dream? (Pay particular attention to anything he or she says.)
   - What in the dream appears to account for this behavior?
   - What images are associated with this behavior in the dream? (Think about the setting, the time, the clothes the person is wearing, and the nature and arrangement of surrounding objects.)

---

- How do I behave in the dream? (Again, pay particular attention to spoken words.)
- What in the dream seems to account for my behavior?
- What images are associated with my behavior in the dream? (Some of the images will be the same as the ones associated with the other person's behavior. Take special note of the images that are *exclusively* associated with your behavior, as well as those that are *exclusively* associated with the other person's behavior.)
- What is the end result of the interaction between me and the other person?

2. Look over each of your responses and ask yourself these questions:
   - Is anything about this aspect of the dream similar to a situation or pattern in my real-life relationship with this person? How is it similar? How is it different?
   - Does this aspect of the dream strongly communicate any message to me about:
     a. what a situation or pattern in my real-life relationship with this person is truly like?
     b. what it could be like?
     c. what I should do about this situation or pattern?
     d. any combination of the above?
     If the answer to a, b, c, or d is "yes," state each message communicated in the clearest terms possible.
   - Given a choice, what change(s) would I like to make in this aspect of the dream? Why?
   - Assuming this dream were a real-life scenario, how could I make the change(s)?

3. If you're convinced by your dreamwork so far that the dream is speaking wisely about your relationship with the other person, answer the following questions:
   - What actions could I *theoretically* take to improve my

behavior, based on what I've learned from the dream? Among all these actions, which would I *like* to try?

- What actions could I *theoretically* take to help X (the other person) improve his or her behavior, based on what I've learned from the dream? Among all these actions, which would I *like* to try?
- What positive changes could I *theoretically* make in the circumstances affecting the relationship, based on what I've learned in the dream? Among all these changes, which would I *like* to try?
- What positive changes could I *theoretically* help X make in the circumstances affecting the relationship, based on what I've learned from the dream? Among all these changes, which would I *like* to try?

## Bringing Dreams into Relationships

Before we apply anything we've learned from a dream to a waking-life relationship, it's wise to consider all the possible consequences of our action. Frequently, the dream suggestion will be a relatively benign one that is unlikely to backfire. When my editor friend inferred from her dream that she should try sitting next to, rather than across from, her troublesome colleague, she was risking very little. The relationship had deteriorated to a stage where she could say, "nothing ventured, nothing gained," and a deftly maneuvered change in seating was not, in itself, a major step to take. In most cases when we follow a dream's advice to work constructively toward cooperation with someone else, our chances of doing the wrong thing are minimal. But if we decide primarily on the basis of a dream to adopt a radical or controversial new approach to a relationship, then we have to prepare ourselves more thoroughly to accept the unexpected.

We need to remind ourselves continually that a specific dream may not be giving us a direct, head-on view of a relationship, but, rather, a corner-of-the-eye view. In other words, it may be exploring the fringe issues of a relationship instead of the central issues. Most experts believe that dreams focus on what remains unexpressed in our waking lives. In regard to our relationships, such material may wind up not being expressed precisely because it concerns relatively minor or tentative issues. This possibility has to be weighed against the opposing possibility that the dream is, indeed, discussing a vital issue in the relationship—one that goes unexpressed because we're unwilling or unable to express it.

Or maybe it goes unexpressed because we don't give ourselves the time to do so. Interpersonal communication over the past forty years has suffered drastically from this problem, thanks to our increasing dependence upon television for entertainment, information, role-modeling, and companionship. Sociologist Richard Scheckel claims in his 1985 book *Intimate Strangers* that people under thirty spend an average of six hours a day watching television and twenty minutes a day in live conversation of a personal nature (New York: Doubleday, p. 288). Given this alarming state of affairs, perhaps the connection between video programming and dreams (suggested earlier in this chapter) will grow even stronger, with one medium feeding the other and shaping its content and format in ever more subtle ways. If so, dreams might eventually transmute our waking-life relationships into mock videodramas cast with video celebrities. Certainly if the average person's dependence on TV increases in the future—and there is every indication it will—there will be even more unattended issues in his or her waking-life relationships that could serve as dream fodder.

In addition to respecting the fact that a dream about a relationship may or may not be reflecting a major issue in the equivalent waking-life relationship, we also need to be cautious about how we link the separate roles in a dream relationship to the separate roles in the equivalent waking-life relationship. The cause-and-effect dynamics may be vastly different in each case. Occasionally, we may experiment by transposing roles in a dream, so that our perception of the other person is entirely the opposite of what that person is really like. For example, as an exercise in self-justification or simply "how it feels," we may dream that our lover is betraying us, when, in fact, we are betraying our lover.

Alternatively, we may cast our dream characters into the same mistaken roles that we tend to give them in our waking life. What we think the other person is doing to us, either in reality or in our dreams, we may actually be doing to ourselves—despite (or even to spite) the other person.

In our waking lives, it's especially difficult to judge whether we're erroneously interpreting our role or the other person's role in a relationship, so careful dreamwork is all the more crucial and has the potential to be all the more valuable. A friend shared with me a dream-related experience that underscores this point:

*One night I had a terrible dream about J___ (my husband). We were both hurrying down a street toward a party. I was lagging behind him, and I started begging him to listen to me. At last he paused and I screamed at him, "I'm sorry, I'm miserable about living here, I'm having trouble with my job," and so forth, a real pouring-out! He listened, but then said he wanted to keep hurrying or we'd be late.*

*When I woke up, which I did right away, I was very upset at his callousness. But later, as I broke down the dream into parts and reviewed them, I realized that the dream was not about his being compassionate or not, but about my need to scream. J___ was much more callous in the dream than he would have been in real life. Also, he wasn't even very clearly drawn in the dream, whereas my character was very well drawn. When I thought about that phrase—"I'm sorry, I'm miserable"—how it had sounded and felt to me, I knew that I was really talking to myself. I was absorbed with my problems and was demanding that he take them on. He couldn't, of course, and I was frustrated. This explained to me why I had been so annoyed and embarrassed by my screaming after him while we were heading down the street.*

*It's hard to explain how I came to see into the true meaning of the dream. It just gradually came to me that this dream, in which my husband was so apparently a villain, was really about me, and I'd just stuck my husband there because he is, after all, part of me.*

While a dream or subsequent dreamwork may not reveal any specific action we might profitably take in a waking-life relationship, it can nevertheless encourage us to attend to that relationship more closely. The more conscious effort we put into examining our interactions with others, the more opportunities we'll discover for improving those interactions. In a technological and individualistic age when close, nourishing relationships are seriously endangered, these opportunities are precious and easy to miss. Our dreams can renew and reinforce our vigilance.

## Experiment: Close Encounters of the Waking Kind

The next time you dream about someone you don't see on a daily basis, take it as a sign to call, write, or visit that person. Treat the exchange as a chance to get "up to date" or closer to each other. You don't have to mention the dream itself, if you think you'd be uncomfortable talking about it (although it's a quick, usually flattering way to explain why you've contacted that person, especially if it's been a long time since the last contact).

As a side effect, your real-life exchange with the person can serve as a healthy counterweight to any dream exchange. It will help you avoid misjudging the meaning of the dream, plus it will keep your most recent impression of that person from being the dream representation. It's also conceivable that there's some reason for contacting this person that your conscious mind didn't register, but your dreaming mind did, which might account for your having the dream in the first place.

If you feel comfortable actually discussing the dream with the other person involved, then be sure not to force an interpretation of the dream onto him or her and not to let him or her force an interpretation onto you. Discuss what individual images and events might mean, using open-ended questions.

Another option is to discuss the dream in the same politic manner with a third party. While this action doesn't put you in direct touch with the specific person represented in your dream, it will give you a fresh slant on your relationship with that person and on what the dream might be saying. It may also enhance your relationship with the third party!

For further directions on "buddy" and group dreamwork procedures, see Chapter Eight.

## Dreams and the Social Contract

We've already considered the need to distinguish the separate roles in a dream relationship from the separate roles in its equivalent waking-life relationship. We should also be aware that relationships play roles with each other, and that the roles they play with each other in reality may not match the roles they play with each other in our dreams.

For example, our waking-life relationship with our spouse may be intricately tied to our relationship with our best friend: When we're having problems with the spouse, we may typically turn to the best friend for solace. We may do the same thing in our dream lives, or we may turn around and vent our frustrations with the "best friend" character on the "spouse" character. The particular dream action we take may yield some new insight into how the two relationships coordinate, or it may not. Your wide-awake self must be the judge.

No relationship exists in a vacuum, and the more we examine dreams about our relationships, the more apparent this becomes. In some cases, a minor relationship in our life falls into the same pattern as a major relationship in our life—so much so that a dream may borrow one set of characters to portray a truth about the other set. While it's important to get the two sets of characters straight, it's even more important to recognize the pattern that's depicted, independent of the characters. Dreams tell us even more about the *general* nature of our relationships than they do about the character of *specific* relationships.

The "I" persona is the common denominator in all of our dream-life or waking-life relationships. It possesses a certain range of talents, attitudes, behaviors, emotions, and experiences that establishes parameters for *any* relationship we may form. Dreams show us this range and make us confront who we were, are, and can be as social entities.

In his 1987 essay, "Night Rule: Dreams as Social Intelligence," Dr. John Wikse, associate academic dean of Shimer College in Waukegan, Illinois, recalls a dream that gave him a beautiful image of the individual moving within his or her social network:

> *I once dreamed that I was swimming in the bloodstream of a large, organic body, moving from person to person among members of a research group to which I belonged. The feeling has remained with me as a guide. In the dream, it was as if each other with whom I was related was a unique organ functioning within the larger body that composed us. As I approached each member of the group I was sometimes repelled backward through the arteries which connected us; at times I remained in peaceful equilibrium; at times there was the feeling of friction within a fluid medium. I realized that this dream had offered me a vantage point on the patterns of conflict in my exchanges with others in my "social body." This standpoint is accessible through dream interpretation. (from* The Variety of Dream Experience, *Ullman and Limmer, eds., New York: Continuum, 1987, p. 196)*

# 6

# Dreams and Problem Solving

FOR SEVERAL NERVE-WRACKING weeks in the spring of 1893, Hermann Hilprecht, professor of Assyrian at the University of Pennsylvania, labored over drawings of two small fragments that had been excavated from the ruins of a Babylonian temple. What were these fragments? How old were they? Gathering all the reference materials on the subject, he deduced that the two scraps belonged to two separate finger rings dating from different periods in history, yet he couldn't be sure. Both objects bore cuneiform letters, but he was unable to decipher either inscription.

One night, Hilprecht fell asleep and dreamed that a "tall thin priest of the old pre-Christian Nippur" led him to the temple and told him this story:

*King Kurigalzu [c. 1300 B.C.] once sent to the temple of Bel, among other articles of agate and lapis lazuli, an inscribed votive cylinder of agate. Then we priests suddenly received the command to make for the statue of the god of Ninib a pair of earrings of agate. We were in great dismay, since there was no agate as raw material at hand. In order to execute the command there was nothing for us to do but cut the votive cylinder into three parts, thus making three rings, each of which contained a portion of the inscription. The first two rings served as earrings for the statue of the god; the two fragments which have given you so much trouble are portions of them. If you will put the two together you will have confirmation of my words. But the third ring you have not found in the course of your excavations and you never will find it. (from Patricia Garfield,* Creative Dreaming, *New York: Simon & Schuster, 1974, pp. 42–43)*

Later, Hilprecht made his first visit to the museum in Constantinople (now Istanbul) where the supposedly unrelated fragments had been stored in separate cases. When he held the two pieces together, they fit perfectly; and for the first time, he could make sense of the inscriptions. Most likely we'll never be able to establish whether the priest's story from his dream is actually true. All that we know for certain is that this dreamer enjoyed high esteem in transatlantic academic circles as a man of probity, honor, and exactitude, and that his dream led him to solve a problem that had defied every other available means of solution.

What are we to make of such a dream? Was it psychic? At a loss to come up with any alternative explanation, Hilprecht was willing to permit publication of his "Nippur priest" dream in *Proceedings of the Society for Psychical Research* (London, 1896)—a bold step for such a conservative man. Was his dream a freak of nature, or was it just an unusually impressive example of a kind of dream that occurs frequently to every dreamer?

Let's look at a similar, slightly less mystifying event that took place a century earlier. The impoverished English poet and artist William Blake, who frequently incorporated his dreams into his work, was desperate to find a cheaper way to produce engravings. Blake had wasted several days in fruitless experimentation when his brother Robert came to him in a dream and described an entirely new and different process of copper engraving. The next day, Blake followed Robert's detailed instructions exactly and, wonder of wonders, he had the answer to his quest.

Blake's dream is more explicable in rational terms than Hilprecht's dream. His deceased advisor was, after all, a close relative —someone Blake had known and loved well during his youth. As for the new engraving process, parts of it may have occurred to Blake subconsciously while he struggled with other possibilities during the preceding days. Nevertheless, that such a novel and complicated procedure should be unveiled to him step by step in a dream is astounding. Is Blake's dream a singular miracle in its own right, or a singular example of the miraculous nature of dreams in general?

Let's consider one more famous revelatory dream before attempting an answer—a dream that lies right on the borderline between the comprehensible and the amazing. It came on a snowy night in 1865 to Friedrich August von Kekulé, who had striven for years to visualize the molecular structure of benzene. Kekulé sat dozing in front of a fire, dreaming as he often did of atoms dancing before his eyes, when the following vision took shape:

> This time the smaller groups (of atoms) kept modestly in the background. My mental eye, rendered more acute by repeated visions of this kind, could now distinguish larger structures, of manifold conformation; long rows, sometimes more closely fitted together; all twining and twisting in snake-like motion. But look! What was that? One of the snakes had seized hold of its own tail and the form whirled mockingly before my eyes. As if by a flash of lightning, I awake.

Kekulé immediately saw that the logical structure of carbon compounds (including benzene) was a closed chain or ring, like the vaguely hexagonal dream image of the snake biting its own tail. His insight led to a revolution in carbon-based, *i.e.*, organic, chemistry and prompted him to advise his scientific colleagues at a convention in 1890: "Let us learn how to dream, gentlemen, and then perhaps we will discover the truth." (This quotation and the previous quotation were taken from *Landscapes of the Night,* Christopher Evans, New York: Simon & Schuster, 1985, pp. 219–220.)

Here we have a breakthrough dream that seems more directly linked to the dreamer's conscious experience prior to sleep. The flames of the real-life fire may easily have influenced Kekulé to dream of masses of jiggling atoms, and the snake picture itself is close in kind to the type of diagrammatical mental images that arise when one consciously ponders a difficult scientific problem. By contrast, the historical saga in Hilprecht's dream and the list of instructions in Blake's dream are far more complex and exotic fabrications. Kekulé wasn't even visited by a magical guide who could announce the solution for what it was. He had to find the solution in a waking-life examination of his dream. Still, his dream is extraordinary.

The three dreams we have just reviewed are legends in the annals of both problem solving and dreaming. When teachers, trainers, or cognitive scientists want to illustrate the value to be gained from nonstructured, uncoerced thinking modes, they cite these examples. When dream scholars, analysts, and researchers seek to advocate the utilitarian importance of dreamwork, they do the same.

Practically speaking, such dreams lie at the far end of the problem-solving spectrum. If they are not actual psychic experiences, they are surely leaps of genius that are best considered creative breakthroughs. For this reason, I have decided to discuss dreams of this type in Chapter Seven, "Dreams and Creativity." However, it is because these dreams are so impressive and, therefore, so inspirational, that I feel obligated to introduce them here, to communicate the wondrous potential dreams have of delivering full-blown solutions to problems. In this chapter as a whole, I prefer to focus on the center of the spectrum. I'd like to show how common it is for dreams to make important and intelligible contributions to any kind of waking-life problem-solving endeavor.

You don't have to be mentally or spiritually gifted to experience helpful dreams, or to translate them into reality when you awake.

There exists an overwhelming body of anecdotal evidence to suggest that dreams are, by nature, problem-solving mechanisms, and down through the ages, people of all stripes have successfully interpreted and implemented solutions that came to them in their dreams. The notion of attending to a problem by "sleeping on it" has become ingrained in the human imagination, and the phrase "dreaming up a solution" has been embedded in virtually every human language.

Some people, of course, take the advice to "sleep on it" more keenly than others. Bertrand Russell, for example, liked to solve an especially recalcitrant problem (which in his case might have been mathematical, philosophical, or political in character) by cramming his brain with as much information as he could gather during the day and then retiring for a long, luxuriant night's sleep. The next morning, he testified, the solution to the problem frequently presented itself with very little effort. Dr. Patricia Garfield, a professional dream researcher and author of the 1974 book *Creative Dreaming,* calls this phenomenon "the principle of subject immersion," and it seems to work involuntarily as well as voluntarily.

Recent scientific studies have confirmed that we tend to dream more intensely and more purposefully when we're undergoing stress or when we're challenged to solve particularly bothersome problems than we do at other times. This could help explain why so many of the dreams we remember are unpleasant. It's only natural, psychologically speaking, that we brood more on the difficulties and mistakes in our lives than we do on the things that come easy or go well.

In the early 1980s Dr. Rosalind Cartwright, chairperson and professor of psychology at Chicago's Rush-Presbyterian–St. Luke's Medical Center, charted the dreams of three groups of women volunteers who agreed to spend regularly scheduled nights in the center's sleep laboratory. One group consisted of women who were happily married, another group consisted of women who were recently divorced and depressed, and the remaining group consisted of women who were divorced and well-adjusted to single life.

Cartwright established not only that dreams are directly affected by major life events, but also that dreams take on a recognizably different pattern depending on the dreamer's state of mind.

When life is proceeding smoothly, according to Cartwright's study, people are generally less aware of their dreams, and the dreams they do remember are usually playful and variable, as if the dreamer were flipping channels on a television set. Under stress, on the other hand, people's dreams become more organized, as if they were tackling problems and trying to resolve them. The nightly dreams of her depressed subjects (*i.e.,* the different dreams that they would typically have in the course of a single night's sleep) all tended to exhibit the same developmental stages: first, a ten-minute dream that set up the problem (a "restatement" dream); then two or more dreams to elaborate the problem at increasingly greater length, often featuring material referring to similar problems in the past; and finally, a dream that tried to bring the problem to a conclusion—the most positive, negative, or confused dream of all.

Now Cartwright has launched a second, much larger study—featuring divorced men as well as divorced women—that is verifying the results of her earlier study. The July 1987 issue of *American Health* singled out the following dream of one of Cartwright's male participants to illustrate the classic pattern that she is once again encountering in the dreams of her most sorely troubled subjects:

> *The first image: He* [the dreamer] *is cleaning out the garage at the house he had lived in with his ex-wife. Then he is standing by the curb, setting out "stuff" he intends to take to his new home. Suddenly, a man in a pickup truck starts to haul the stuff away. The dreamer protests but the other man says, "You put this stuff out here, so anybody can take it." The dreamer picks up a chair and starts to hit the intruder.*

In subsequent therapy sessions attached to the study, the dreamer was able to appreciate that the "stuff" he didn't want to leave behind was his children. The chance that another man might become a father figure to them was suddenly clarified as the factor in the dreamer's new life that was the most difficult for him to accept. His dream did not present a very effective solution to the problem, but it indicated what the problem was, rehearsed where his feelings about the problem were possibly leading him, and spurred him to deal with the problem more maturely.

In a different but equally intriguing experiment, Cartwright presented a mixed set of volunteers with sample life problems, such as situations involving sexual guilt or conflicts between business and pleasure. They were asked to offer their solutions to these hypothetical dilemmas seven hours later. In the meantime, half of the volunteers remained awake, while the other half slept in the laboratory—some awakened whenever they registered REM sleep and some not. The problem solutions given by the group that had been allowed to dream were noticeably more realistic, comprehensive, and attractive than those given by the two groups who hadn't dreamed.

What both the Cartwright experiments and the anecdotal evidence tell us is that our dreams respond to our problems in an automatic fashion. Whether it is the express biological and psychological function of dreams to engage in problem solving has so far resisted proof, but that dreaming can have a positive influence on problem solving has been demonstrated inside as well as outside the laboratory.

## Setting Problem Solving Goals

In real life, dreams can assist us to solve major and minor problems alike. The secret lies in the dreaming mind's capacity to generate multitudes of high-impact images associated with a given problem that we can use to understand and manage that problem more effectively. Most of these images are essentially visual, but many appeal to one or more of the other senses as well. This multimodal material gives us a better *feeling* for a problem, particularly one that is highly verbal or conceptual in nature.

When we're faced with the common, day-to-day problem of deciding what we want to eat, we run through a variety of foods in our minds and picture them, smell them, taste them, and sometimes even feel and hear them (hence the advertising dictum, "Sell the sizzle, not the steak"). When we're faced with a much larger and more abstract problem, such as what to do about a crisis at work, we instinctively try to do the same thing—*sense* possible solutions—but the lack of a readily available repertoire of images often inhibits our progress.

Our dreaming minds are not nearly so inhibited. They pour out images that pertain to our daily conflicts. True, we may not be able to draw the connections without some effort; but that very effort can keep us moving toward a solution. Jean Wolff, the owner of East Side, West Side, a popular restaurant in Boston, believes that the attention she paid to a singularly vivid dream helped her to keep her initial business venture from financial collapse. Here is her story:

*My first place, a French restaurant in a converted factory space, was not doing well at all. The food was good, the prices were' right, and I had some loyal regulars, but it wasn't pulling in the volume I needed to keep it going. I was panicky, and then I had a strange dream.*

*In the dream, I was at a party wearing this outfit that was extremely stylish but also made me feel extremely uncomfortable, physically and emotionally. Like a lot of high fashion, it was one of those outfits that seem fascinating one minute and ridiculous the next. Then I noticed this woman across the room who was dressed so simply and yet so beautifully. I suspected that she was laughing at me, and I was mortified. I started to leave but then she hurried up to me and said, "What's the matter?"*

*That's the dream. The more I thought about it, the more I felt that the outfit stood for the way I'd put together the restaurant—out of ideas I'd borrowed from what you might call "high fashion" experts. A couple of days later I recognized that the woman in my dream was one of my*

> *regular customers: not a beautiful dresser necessarily but a person I'd come to like and respect. I decided then and there to ask her opinion, as a customer, about what would improve the restaurant. I couldn't have made a better move. She went out to eat a lot and several times in her life she'd been a waitress. She had some terrific ideas about making the place more personal and cozy; and after I took her advice, business started picking up right away.*

Dream imagery geared toward problem solving can also be brief and to the point. All the dreamer has to do is pay attention and take appropriate action. Dr. William C. Dement, a leading American researcher of sleep and dreams at Stanford University, reports that professional golfer Jack Nicklaus once dreamed he was holding his club in a different manner and thereby greatly improving his swing. Over the next few weeks Nicklaus experimented with the new grip he'd learned in his dream, and it worked well enough to pull his career out of a year-long slump.

One time in graduate school when I was worried about meeting a deadline for a term paper, I dreamed that I was sitting in a resort lounge with a window view of a lake, proofreading a finished manuscript. The next day, I began thinking about the possibility of going off to some quiet place where I could concentrate on finishing my report. Ordinarily I would have dismissed the idea instantly. It would have seemed too disruptive of my overall schedule and too expensive, both in terms of the cost of the venture itself and the income I'd lose by not driving my cab while I was away. Besides, I didn't know of any place nearby like the one I'd envisioned. The dream, however, gave me the incentive to ask about such a retreat among my student friends. One of them said I could use his family's hunting lodge in Maine for free, so I grabbed the opportunity. It was very primitive and didn't have a view of a lake, but it was private and peaceful. I had no trouble finishing my report; in fact, I enjoyed doing it.

Now it's time for you to examine images derived from your waking life that can help you set up problem-solving goals and work effectively toward achieving them. This intentional, image-based approach (popularly called "visualization," although the term refers only to one sense) is similar to the direction that dreams take when they process information. The more you reflect on important details in your conscious experience, the better you become at identifying significant details in your dreams.

When you answer each of the following questions, try to "live" or revivify the incidents they bring to mind, if only for a few seconds. It may be easier to respond to the more general questions by focusing them on one arena of your life at a time, such as work, education, relationships, leisure activities, health, possessions, household management.

- **What have been some of the toughest problems you've faced in your life?**
  For each specific problem that you recall, ask yourself:
  - What made this problem so difficult?
  - How did I solve (or manage) this problem?
  - What factors were involved in choosing this particular strategy?
  - What were the positive and negative results of this strategy?
  - How might I have solved (or managed) this problem more effectively?

- **What have been some of the easiest-to-handle problems you've faced in your life?**
  For each specific problem, ask yourself:
  - What made this problem so easy to handle?
  - How did I solve (or manage) this problem?
  - What factors were involved in choosing this particular strategy?
  - How might I have solved (or managed) this problem more effectively?

■ **What kinds of problems do you repeatedly face?**
For each specific kind of problem, ask yourself:

- Why am I repeatedly faced with this kind of problem?
- How do I usually solve (or manage) it?
- What are the positive and negative results of this strategy?
- How might I solve (or manage) it more effectively?
- How might I change things so that I would face this kind of problem less often?

■ **What patterns exist in the way you go about solving (or managing) problems?**
For each pattern, ask yourself:

- Why do I follow this pattern?
- What are the positive and negative aspects of this pattern?
- How could I improve this pattern?
- What other basic strategies could I adopt to supplement or replace this pattern?

■ **What specific problems are you most interested in solving (or managing) now or in the near future?**
For each problem, ask yourself:

- Why is this problem so important to me?
- What is its history (that is, its background, causes, and effects)?
- What would the result be if I could solve (or manage) this problem successfully?
- What are the various ways in which I could solve (or manage) it?
- What are the possible weaknesses and strengths of each strategy?
- What possible obstacles or opportunities now or in the near future might affect the way I solve (or manage) this problem?

Through performing this exercise in guided imagery, we gradually learn that the term "problem solving" is a misnomer for a process that is much more complex. Before we can tackle any problem, we need to be sure we understand it thoroughly. In many cases, this is the real challenge of problem solving: not *fixing* what's wrong, but *figuring out* what's wrong.

Suppose you consistently have trouble doing all the things you want or need to do during the week. You may decide that your basic problem lies in scheduling, so you'll draw up elaborate "to-do" lists and maybe even buy a wrist alarm. In fact, your basic problem may be that you're trying to do too much, that you lack motivation, that you aren't allowing others to help you, or that you suffer from physical or emotional debilitation. Until you're able to establish more clearly what issues are the most critical ones, not just the most obvious ones, your chances of success are seriously undermined.

We also need to acknowledge that not every problem can be solved. Some tricky situations can be overcome, minimized, coped with, or avoided, but if we persist in trying to solve them, we'll only be wasting our very limited time, energy, and resources. This is almost always the case in troublesome interpersonal relationships. If your spouse doesn't behave the way you want him or her to behave, for example, it's a good idea to try to understand all the factors contributing to that behavior (as well as your own) and then experiment with techniques aimed at modifying your spouse's behavior (as well as your own), such as serious talks, incentive-and-reward systems, or changes in lifestyle. Whatever you do, however, it's unrealistic and possibly damaging to harbor the expectation that the problem between you and your spouse, as you perceive it, will vanish altogether.

"Problem solving" is such a highly compressed expression that it encourages us to rush for a "right" answer, instead of making the slower but surer effort first to understand a problem thoroughly and then to choose wisely among a number of possible options.

Unfortunately, this rush-for-the-right-answer mentality does a great deal of damage. As I mentioned in Chapter Three (where I discussed the rush for the right answer in the context of dream interpretation), it causes a large percentage of students in American educational systems to stumble and quit the race. It also gives many adults in high-pressure jobs a bad attitude about digressive activities like imagining and dreaming, which can actually be uniquely productive.

To avoid the pitfalls of rushing for the right answer, it's best to think of problem solving as an operation consisting of two successive stages: "problem analyzing" and "decision making." Here are the actual steps involved in each of these stages:

## Problem Analyzing

1. Research the "problem environment," learning all you can about the circumstances surrounding the problem and taking into account all possible causes and effects.
2. Define as precisely as possible what the problem is.
3. Develop a list of all the possible ways of solving (or managing) this problem.
4. Identify goals that you seek to attain by solving (or managing) the problem.
5. Develop decision criteria based on these goals: specific results that you want to achieve by way of your solution to (or management of) the problem.

## Decision Making

6. Research the "decision environment," learning all you can about the resources you can apply to solving or managing the problem, the opportunities and constraints facing you, and the pos-

sible consequences of different courses of action (see step three)—given all the factors both inside and outside your control.

7. Establish methods for solving (or managing) the problem that seem the most feasible, given your research.

8. Choose the alternative that best fulfills the decision criteria (see step five).

9. Devise plans for following through on this course of action that will allow you to tell if and when you're making progress.

So now we have a cold, clear outline of the entire *rational* process that lies behind the term "problem solving." One of the main values of dreams is that they can supply *irrational* input into our problem-solving endeavors. The dreaming mind works with information in ways that are difficult if not impossible for the conscious mind to duplicate, and therefore, it assists us to penetrate the "unknown" elements associated with any baffling problem or hypothetical course of action: things we're overlooking, things we're afraid to face, things we suspect but can't quite express.

I believe those artists of the English language whom we call "romantic" do the best job of describing what the dreaming mind does to facilitate problem solving. Dreams give us what the poet John Keats calls "negative capability," so that we are "capable of being in uncertainties, mysteries, and doubts, without any irritable reaching after facts and reason." Dreams constitute what the poet Samuel Taylor Coleridge calls "the secondary imagination," which "dissolves, diffuses, and dissipates in order to recreate." Dreams exhibit what the fiction writer F. Scott Fitzgerald classifies as genius: "the ability to hold two opposed ideas in the mind at the same time and still retain the capacity to function." In summary, our dreams are able to converse more freely than our rational minds about the ambiguous situations in our lives, and there is much we can learn about our problems and problem-solving options if we listen to this conversation more closely.

## Looking Before You Leap: The "Flapper" Dream

In Part Three of Jonathan Swift's *Gulliver's Travels*, Gulliver visits Laputa, a flying island populated by scientists, mathematicians, and philosophers. His curiosity is immediately aroused by their unusual companions:

> *I observed, here and there, many in the habit of servants, with a blown bladder fastened like a flail to the end of a short stick, which they carried in their hands. In each bladder was a small quantity of dried pease, or little pebbles (as I was afterwards informed). With these bladders they now and then flapped the mouths and ears of those who stood near them, of which practice I could not then conceive the meaning; it seems, the minds of these people are so taken up with intense speculations, that they neither can speak, nor attend to the discourses of others, without being roused by some external taction upon the organs of speech and hearing; for which reason, those persons, who are able to afford it always keep a flapper (the original is* climenole*), in their family, as one of their domestics. . . . This flapper is likewise employed diligently to attend his master in his walks, and, upon occasion, to give him a soft flap on the eyes, because he is always so wrapped up in cogitation that he is in manifest danger of falling down every precipice, and bouncing his head against every post; and in the streets, of jostling others, or being jostled himself, into the kennel. (from Jonathan Swift,* Gulliver's Travels, *New York: Crown, 1985, pp. 149–150)*

During times when we're undergoing challenges in our lives, our dreams often act as our flappers. They force us to attend to matters that we're too distracted to address as we go about our real-world business. They make us sense aspects related to complicated situations that are not being covered by our waking-life "cogitations" and "speculations." They alert us to crises and obstacles along the way that our five physical senses are not consciously registering. And they point to possible solutions that may otherwise be too dim or too dazzling to detect.

Often the "flap" in a dream takes the form of an object lesson: a provocative picture, puzzle, or exercise that recasts the problem and forces the dreamer to come to terms with it. Dr. Martin E. P. Seligman, a psychologist at the University of Pennsylvania, is one of the foremost authorities today who believes that dreams may perform an important physiological function by serving as test vehicles for framing and, ultimately, managing difficult mental and emotional tasks. In discussing REM sleep in general, Seligman comments:

> Perhaps it provides practice at the cognitive synthesis we must perform each day of our lives, by allowing us to rehearse, through our dreams, the ability to make disparate images and feelings cohere. Infants, who sleep ten to twelve hours a day, would thus have ample practice in this skill.

Major life crises are capable of throwing us into a state of childlike helplessness; and in this state, we may well tap our dreaming genius for help. A friend recently separated from her husband and, in the process, dissolved her business association with him. Faced with an uncertain future, she experienced the following "test vehicle" dream: one that features a crossroad, which (like a classroom, a trial, a competition, a game, or an exhibition) is an image that frequently appears in dreams associated with problem solving:

> I am walking up a bare, deserted hill on a paved road. I look below and see the lights of Phoenix, a city where I lived a carefree, vagabond life for several years. The lights are pretty; but as I look at them, I hear the sounds of traffic more and more distinctly and soon I can make out smoke drifting across them. I look away. Ahead of me, the road forks in three directions. On the left, it runs in a straight line uphill toward a big, shiny

*bakery plant. People are streaming in, chatting as they go. I turn my head so they won't notice me and wonder who I am. On the right, the road meanders downhill to the home of a friend of mine who runs a day-care center and studies meditation. I'm tempted to go visit her, but I suddenly spot her moving around inside and I lose my desire to visit. Ahead of me, the road levels off. I see a grove of pine trees. In the center of the grove are stacks of soft pine wood and tools lying everywhere. I hurry to claim this spot.*

This dream neatly frames the dreamer's four choices (and, in fact, goes beyond presenting the choices to advising the dreamer which choice to make):

1. She could live the same type of aimless, day-to-day existence she once knew in Phoenix. The dream suggests that such a life might be full of dazzling moments, but it would ultimately lead to more and more jarring noises and smoky confusion.
2. She could give her life structure, productivity, and social contacts by taking a conventional business job (as symbolized by the bakery plant). Her behavior in the dream indicates that there is a strong conflict between this possible lifestyle and who she really is.
3. She could model her life after her friend's life, which seems attractively domestic and peaceful, and yet when she takes a closer look at this life in the dream, it doesn't appear so desirable.
4. She could build a new kind of life altogether (as symbolized by the fresh wood and tools). The fact that she moves swiftly in the dream to claim the spot among the pine trees suggests that this choice is the most attractive and "natural" of the four.

In addition to helping us cope with emotional problems, dreams also can assist us to solve problems that are more practical or intellectual in nature. During 1987 and 1988, I interviewed several industrial plant owners as part of my research for a book on business espionage. One of them told me about a nightmare he had that enlightened him about a serious security risk in his area of responsibility:

*I was visiting one of my line managers at his home. He took me into his backyard to show me a big network of ponds and waterfalls he'd created there. I didn't think it looked very good. Water was flowing everywhere in dirt ditches with small dirt walls to keep it from running over. I thought that there should be fewer ditches and that the walls should be more substantial and more decorative; but I didn't want to hurt his feelings by saying anything critical. He turned up the water to show me the full effect of the waterfalls and all hell broke loose. Valves busted and water started pouring in. All at once the ground below our feet was too mushy for us to move. I was sure I was going to drown and woke up in a panic.*

Back at the plant, the owner took special note of the manager's office, a free-standing room with glass walls on each side that stood in the center of a huge, bustling assembly hangar. As he continued his observation, one employee entered and left the empty, unlocked office to make a phone call, and the owner thought to himself, "That guy could see or take any papers he wanted while he was in there!" He recalled his dream and was suddenly struck by the existence of a major problem: His manager's office was a wide-open target for every spy who wanted to steal important business secrets, whether the spy was an unscrupulous employee or an outside agent posing as a supplier, a consultant, or a tour-group member. In short, the manager's private "turf" was a major source of "leaks"!

The plant owner may have been subconsciously accumulating evidence for quite a while about the vulnerability of his manager's office. Because the plant did a great deal of government contract work and often developed innovative ways to improve routine assembly procedures, the owner had to be continually concerned about security issues. Nevertheless, he'd failed to put together this specific body of evidence until he was inspired by his dream to do so. The owner subsequently counseled the manager about restricting access to his office, replaced the glass walls with see-through mirrors, installed outside phones and photocopying equipment for employee use, and taking a cue from his dream, color-coded the hangar floor with highly visible pathways beyond which visitors were not permitted to stray.

On certain memorable occasions, the "flap" in a dream takes the form of a positive awakening, an "aha!" slap on the forehead. Once I was having difficulties writing a script for an educational videotape program. Although I was pleased with my own arrangement of teaching points, the producers of the tape kept hedging, saying that the script didn't seem "deep" enough for the audience. I kept adding more sophisticated points, making the script larger and more complex; but the producers still came back with the same criticism, "Not deep enough." In time, I grew very frustrated over their inability to be more specific. For once, it didn't help to remind myself that nonwriting employers might not need a writer at all if they were capable of expressing themselves more specifically. I was completely stumped about what my producers wanted, and, much worse, so were they.

One night I dreamed that an unusual mobile home was parked across the street in front of my apartment building, blocking traffic. It was trimmed to look like a medieval castle and was surprisingly attractive. I walked over and peered into one of the windows. There, on a stand, sat an open book, beautifully bordered and ornamented with detailed scrollwork. Suddenly I realized it was a Jefferson Bible, a type of Bible invented by Thomas Jefferson in which all the words of Jesus (*i.e.,* the most important words) are printed in red instead of black. I noticed that these red words seemed very deeply embossed into the page.

The next morning I knew right away that the dream had some bearing on my problem with the script. I'd been thinking about little else for several weeks in a row, of course, but there were also other clues: The dream featured a trailer parked in a street—an image I would be quick to associate with a videotape production —plus a book I identified as a "Bible," which is a term often applied to the script of a videotape.

I decided to practice what the dream seemed to be preaching. I underscored the main teaching points in the script and cut out the others, which had always bothered me despite the fact that they made the script technically "deeper." Then I concentrated on strengthening these major ideas by embellishing them: restating them in different ways, providing a greater number of scencs to exemplify them, and in general calling attention to them more impressively. As fate would have it, the producers loved the revised script. What I considered "basic and repetitive," they considered "deep"—a truth only my dream succeeded in communicating.

---

## Experiment: Night School

"Flapper" dreams, as we've just seen, come in a variety of formats. Some of them, like the crossroad dream, offer symbolic depictions that we can immediately relate to waking-life problems. Others, such as the back yard waterworks and Jefferson Bible dreams, are more obscure. Either they present us with a problem that's several steps removed from its real-life equivalent (the back yard waterworks dream) or they tantalize us with a single vivid image that we may or may not be able to connect to a real-life problem, depending on how much conscious thought we give to the problem when we're awake.

To learn from any of these "flapper" dreams, we need to consider them as educational puzzles, analogous to poems that we might explicate in a literature course, frogs we might dissect in a biology course, or equations we might work out in a mathematics course. If you want to establish whether a suspiciously nagging dream or dream image is, in fact, dealing with a problem that exists in your waking life, answer the following questions and take the appropriate analytical action, based on your response:

---

■ **Does the plot of the dream concern a problem (include any conflict or competition in this category)? If so:**

1. State the opposing sides of the problem as succinctly as possible. Depending on the dream, these sides may be expressed as one person versus another person, one person versus a situation, one situation versus another situation, and so forth. There can, of course, be more than two sides to a problem. If the dream contains two or more separate problems, handle each one individually. Later on, you may find that they interrelate.

2. Look at the environment surrounding the problem *(i.e.,* the people, places, events, objects, and behavior). Note all the actual and possible causes and effects of the problem. Examine the factors that become associated with the problem as it develops. Think of possible long-range consequences of the problem that can be inferred from the dream.

3. Identify solutions to the problem. If any solutions are tried in the dream, determine why they are tried and why they succeed or fail. Think of possible solutions to the problem that can be inferred from the dream.

4. List the major problems (including conflicts or competitions) that you are currently facing in your waking life. For each problem, consider the opposing sides, the problem environment (causes, effects, associations, long-range consequences), and the possible solutions; then, draw any connections you can between this problem and the problem in your dream.

5. Using the dream as a starting point, think of all the actual or potential problems in your waking life that it is capable of representing. In other words, think of problems that do or

could have similar opposing sides, environments, or possible solutions.

6. Based on your rational and intuitive responses to steps four and five, decide which waking-life problem (if any) your dream is addressing.

■ **Does the dream contain a particularly arresting image? If so:**

1. Look at the image carefully and establish any contrasting elements among its component features. Consider its different parts, colors, textures, shapes, volumes, designs, styles, functions, and so forth. Think also about ways in which it is familiar as opposed to ways in which it is strange.

2. Look at the environment surrounding the image. Examine what is (or might be) responsible for creating the image. Think about the factors that are associated with the image in its present, arresting form. Think about the potential future of this image (possibilities of change, use, or impact) based on what you can infer from the dream.

3. Create an image in your mind that represents the opposite of this dream image. (You may be able to create several different images that are, in different ways, opposites of this dream image.) It's often easier to relate an image of this type to your waking-life problem than the dream image itself; especially if the dream image is presenting a positive solution (as yet unrealized) that reverses a negative situation (already realized).

4. List the major problems (including conflicts and competitions) that you are currently facing in your waking life. For each problem, consider the opposing sides, the problem envi-

ronment (causes, effects, associations, long-range consequences) and the possible solutions; then, draw any connections you can between this problem and the arresting image
in your dream or any opposite image you have created (see
step three).

5. Using the dream image as a starting point, think of all the
actual or potential problems in your waking life to which it
may be referring. Then use an opposing image you have
created (see step three) and perform the same activity.

## Incubating a Dream

We don't have to wait passively, night after night, for a dream that
will shed light on our problems. We can actually will such a dream
to appear. It's a simple matter of autosuggestion. If we believe in
the ability of dreams to discuss waking-life problems, and if we
develop a sense of how our dreams in general go about doing this,
it's not difficult at all to proceed one step further and prepare our
dreaming mind to address the material we want it to address.
Psychological and intellectual prompting works to shape conscious
thinking, and it also works to shape dream thinking.

In ancient times, it was common practice to ask for a dream
and to perform "rituals of intention" that reinforced the serious-
ness of the request. The earliest record we have of this kind of
personal ceremony is an instruction written on an Egyptian pa-
pyrus dating from around 2000 B.C., now on exhibit in the
British Museum:

*To obtain a vision from the god Besa* [guardian of mysteries], *make a
drawing of Besa on your left hand and, enveloping your hand in a strip of
black cloth that has been consecrated to Isis, lie down to sleep without
speaking a word, even in answer to a question.*

Greeks in the sixth century B.C. institutionalized dream seeking as a religious rite. Pilgrims who wished to experience a certain type of dream would spend the night sleeping in a temple dedicated to the appropriate god. Asklepios, the god of healing, rapidly gained a credible reputation for delivering diagnostic and even curative dreams, and his temple at Epidaurus became the focus of an enormous cult that thrived until it was rigorously suppressed in the fifth century A.D. by Constantine, the first Roman emperor to embrace Christianity.

Today, the act of intentionally programming dreams ahead of time is known as dream incubation, and one of its more enthusiastic proponents is Dr. Henry Reed, who frequently conducts dream incubation workshops and experiments under the auspices of the Association for Research and Enlightenment in Virginia Beach, Virginia. According to Reed, "Symbolic ritual might be a helpful method for people to assimilate the transformative power of their dreams," so he usually creates a ceremonial structure for his group members to follow on their dream incubation nights.

In one weekend gathering, for example, Reed asked participants to bring small tents. Each incubant was then directed to visualize, from memory, someone very wise and to imagine that the tent was a sanctuary located in a place he or she considered to be peaceful and special. Throughout the day, Reed directed each incubant in role-playing activities with his or her wise person concerning the problem to be incubated; and at night, each incubant slept in his or her tent to have a helpful dream.

Reed's most famous and ambitious dream-incubation project in recent years has been the series of "dream-helper" experiments he devised with fellow psychologist Dr. Robert Van de Castle, a professor in the department of behavioral medicine at the University of Virginia Medical School and the director of its Nocturnal Cognition Laboratory. The two-day "dream-helper" experiment consists of the following protocol: A group of people are directed to focus their dreams on a single group member and his or her problem (which is not stated). During the day before they dream, the group members spend time together—including meditative time—so that everyone may come to know the target individual better. The following morning, the group members gather in one place and share their dreams. Details that are similar from dream to dream are noted, and the target individual is asked if and how these images connect with his or her problem.

Reed and Van de Castle have testified to some remarkable insights arising from these experiments. In one session, each group member dreamed of a water image; and the target individual did, indeed, have a severe phobia of water. Working with the specific water images that the group gave her, she was able to understand more clearly how she acquired the phobia and to develop the resolve to take swimming lessons. In another session, several group members said that they had dreamed of objects whizzing through the air. The target individual, a shy, doubtful woman, reacted violently to this news. She had been brooding over her unhappy childhood, and the dream reports precipitated a breakthrough memory of how her stepbrother and stepsister had thrown rocks at her almost every day as she walked home from school.

It is impossible to explain why the "dream-helper" experiments are so often as successful as they are. Do the helpers pick up subliminal clues from the target individual during the day before the dream? Do individual group members become telepathically linked? Is some aspect of mob psychology or clairvoyance involved? Perhaps someday we'll know. In the meantime, the fact remains that the process works, and it is helpful. I mention it here only to show how far-reaching the application of incubated dreams to problem solving can be.

A more practical but equally fascinating overnight experiment in dream incubation was conducted in 1980 by Dr. William C. Dement at Stanford University. In this case, five hundred undergraduate students were involved—a much broader range of subjects than Reed or Van de Castle used—including people who had little or no interest in dreams. Dement posed the following problem to his volunteers: "The letters O, T, T, F, F . . . form the beginning of a sequence. Find a simple rule for determining any or all success-ive letters. According to your rule, what would be the next two letters of the sequence?" He also gave his volunteers a questionn-aire on which they were to discuss any dreams they had that night.

The next day, Dement collected and collated the questionnaires of those students who recorded both an answer to the problem and at least one dream. He discovered that nine students could recall dreams that presented the correct solution. Two of these nine students had figured out the solution before going to bed, so that left seven students who literally solved the problem in a dream. Here is one of those dreams:

> *I was standing in an art gallery, looking at the paintings on the wall. As I walked down the hall, I began to count the paintings: one, two, three, four, five. But as I came to the sixth and seventh, the paintings had been ripped from their frames. I stared at the empty frames with a peculiar feeling that some mystery was about to be solved. Suddenly I realized that the sixth and seventh spaces were the solution to the problem!*

The solution to the problem was that the given sequence repre-sented the first letters of "one, two, three, four, five," so the next two items in the sequence would logically be "s" (for "six") and "s" (for "seven").

In another, more spontaneous experiment, Dement asked some of his students to come up with a one-word solution to the letters H, I, J, K, L, M, N, O and to record their dreams that night. One man wrote back:

> *I had several dreams, all of which had water in them somewhere. In one dream I was hunting for sharks. In another I was confronted by a barracuda while skin diving. In another dream it was raining heavily. In another I was sailing into the wind.*

The writer offered the word "alphabet" as his solution; but the answer Dement originally had in mind was "water," because H-to-O or $H_2O$ is the chemical notation for water.

Dr. Morton Schatzman, an American psychiatrist based in London, decided to try a series of similar experiments during the summer and fall of 1983 with readers of the prestigious British journal *New Scientist*. In the June issue, he asked, "What is remarkable about the following sentence? 'I am not very happy acting pleased whenever prominent scientists overmagnify intellectual enlightenment.'" Among the "positive" replies published in the August issue was this one:

> *Before I went to bed I read the sentence ten times. That night I had the following dream:*
>
> *I am giving a lecture to a number of scientists about hypnosis. They are seated at round tables scattered about a large hall. Nobody is listening to me. This makes me very angry, and I shout, "I am not very happy!" The scientists seated at the tables nearest to me look up. I wake up.*
>
> *It suddenly struck me that the scientists who had responded to me were seated at five separate tables with one scientist at the table nearest to me, two at another table, three at a third table, and so on up to five. I began to feel that numbers were important in this problem, and I counted the number of words in the sentence. As I did so, I realised that it was the number of letters in each word that was important. I counted the letters and arrived at the sequence 1 ("I"), 2 ("am"), 3 ("not")... 13 ("enlightenment").*

Commenting on his experiment, Schatzman said:

> *Anecdotes about problem-solving dreams hardly constitute evidence that all dreams contribute to problem solving (or have that as their purpose), but the anecdotes illustrate that at least some dreams do.... For practical purposes, perhaps the most important question is: if you examine your dreams as well as the thoughts in your waking life for answers to prob-*

*lems, do you have a better chance of finding the answers than if you examine only your waking-life thoughts? (This and the quotation above are from Dr. Morton Schatzman, "Solve Your Problems in Your Sleep,"* New Scientist, *August 1983, p. 692.)*

Even in the very pragmatic world of business, dream incubation has its place. Francis Menezes, an internationally renowned management trainer, demonstrated this in 1987, when he was hired by a gigantic chemical manufacturing firm owned by the government of India to solve a morale problem in its research and development department. Menezes invited fifty-two scientists from the department to spend three days and three nights at a comfortable estate in Poona, India. After dinner each evening, Menezes asked the scientists to think of a workplace problem that bothered them, summarize it in a single phrase, write that phrase on a sheet of paper, and insert the paper in an envelope. As they lay down in bed, next to the envelope, they were requested to concentrate on the phrase they had written, with the intention of dreaming about it.

Each morning after the first night, almost all the scientists (including the self-proclaimed skeptics) announced that they had experienced surprisingly revealing dreams about their work-related problems. One scientist, for example, found himself haranguing one of his most accomplished peers; another scientist pelted his unappreciative boss with lab equipment. Menezes recorded and analyzed all the dreams and made appropriate recommendations to the firm's top executives. They were so impressed with the findings that they inaugurated a number of changes designed to promote better internal communications, more productive research teams, and more flexible working conditions. Independently, most of the scientists who had participated in the training seminar started their own weekly meetings to discuss their past week's dreams and set up incubation objectives for the week to come.

Many citizens of the business world, increasingly caught up in corporate bureaucracy and politics as their careers progress, tend to lose a major part of their curiosity, resourcefulness, and initiative. Menezes believes that individual as well as group dreamwork based on dream incubation can repair some of the damage. "Dreams are always urging us toward greater wholeness," he explains. "As such, they can be a very important instrument for change" (*The Omni WholeMind Newsletter,* October 1987).

Dream incubation also helps to resolve the tensions that dreamwork trainers themselves experience. Will Phillips, a consultant based in Orlando, Florida, was once especially nervous about a demonstration he was preparing for the members of a local business organization. Using two battery-operated toy trucks, one bearing a heart symbol and the other bearing a lightbulb symbol, he hoped to dramatize how dreamwork can bring the heart (instincts) and the head (intellect) together. The props fed his speech very nicely, but he was worried that the gimmick as a whole might be too culturally jarring for his audience. The night before the engagement, he asked for guidance from his dreams. Here is the dream that followed, as recounted in the November-December 1987 issue of *Dream Network Bulletin:*

> *I dreamed of playing outside in the ice and snow with some new friends. For fun, we began building ice slides, like bobsled runs, with elaborate twists and turns. As we became comfortable with the speed, we began developing and performing fancy stunts. It was lots of fun, but also involved a fairly high degree of risk. After one particularly dangerous stunt ended with a frightening near-collision, I decided to quit. But a good friend approached me and encouraged me to keep practicing. He sincerely believed that we could do anything if we persevered. His courage inspired me to go back and try again.*

When Phillips arrived at the banquet hall for his speech the next evening, the host—a man named Henry—greeted him and privately expressed his concern that a talk about dreams might not relate well to a group of rather conservative business executives. Phillips recalls:

*In my mind, I envisioned Henry keeling over of a heart attack as I brought my toy trucks into the banquet hall. I felt a powerful urge to excuse myself to the men's room and crawl out of the window. Then I remembered my dream: playing games with new friends in a cold environment and being inspired by my friend's courage to persevere in spite of my fears. I knew that I had to act on the dream.*

Phillips's talk was warmly received. A lengthy question-and-answer session ensued, and he signed up a number of new participants for his workshops. "To my even greater satisfaction," he confessed, "Henry told me that he was really going to try to remember a dream."

---

## Experiment: Dream Engineering

The next time you need help working out a problem in your life—whether it's an academic problem or a more practical problem involving work, school, home, leisure, health, or relationships—try asking for guidance from a dream. Here is a basic dream-incubation procedure you can follow:

1. Several times during the day before your dream, devote a few minutes to thinking about the problem: its causes, effects, environment, and possible solutions. Tell yourself that you intend to dream about this problem, and that by taking this time to think about it, you are preparing yourself for the dream.

2. Before you retire for the night, boil your thoughts down to one short phrase. You might for example, come up with a statement of the topic about which you want to dream, or a very open-ended question to which you want a response (an open-ended question is one that can't be answered "yes" or "no").

---

3. Write this phrase down in your dream journal or on a piece of paper. Then put the journal or paper and a pencil close to your bed, where you can reach them easily.

4. Repeat the phrase to yourself as you fall asleep, mindful that you want a dream that addresses it.

5. If you wake up during the night, lie still and try to remember any dream you've had so far. If you can reconstruct *any* dream, write it down in your journal or on your piece of paper. If you can't, repeat the phrase to yourself as you start to fall asleep again, mindful that you want a dream that addresses it.

6. When you wake up in the morning, lie still and try to remember any dreams you've had during the night. If you can reconstruct *any* dream, write it down *immediately* in your journal or on your piece of paper and note any relevance that you feel it may have to the target problem. At different times during the following day, devote a few minutes to thinking about the possible relationships between your dream(s) the previous night and the target problem.

It may take several times before an incubation experiment works: For any number of reasons, you may not recall a dream on a given night, or you may not be able to draw any connection between a dream on that night and your target problem. Keep trying, however; when incubation does work, it's particularly satisfying—as if the dream in itself has already begun resolving the problem.

In the spirit of Dr. Henry Reed, you may want to add your own personal ceremonial structure to the incubation process. Any gesture on your part to acknowledge that you intend to incubate a dream is likely to reinforce your mental preparation for that dream. Some people I know formally meditate on the target problem the day before the dream night; or they use a special pillowcase that night to give them a tactile reminder that they intend to dream about a particular issue; or they use a ball of aromatic herbs to give them an olfactory reminder.

## Dream Decision Making

Earlier in this chapter, we examined an important distinction between problem analyzing and decision making, namely, that they are two separate stages in a complete problem-solving process—the former involving estimation, testing, study, and theorizing, and the latter involving judgment and commitment. Up to this point, we've been mostly concerned with problem situations that illustrated both stages of the process. Before leaving the topic of dreams and problem solving, we should consider those problem situations in which the main difficulty is not figuring out *what* the problem is or *how* to solve it but, rather, deciding *which* solution to choose among two or more equally viable alternatives.

Many circumstances in life present us with an array of options that we're unable to narrow down by exercising our analytical skills and referring to our overall goals. While no decision is entirely arbitrary (each alternative having its own set of possibilities and limitations), we're often in a position where we can't argue the case for one choice over another on the grounds of logic. Instead, we must listen to our inner voice: What do we *really* want to do?

For most of us, this consultation is far more difficult than it seems. Our inner voice is ever in competition with other, less authentic but louder voices that make us doubt our ability to make the "right" decision. There are the eloquent voices of outside authorities that tell us what we *should* want, whether we ask them to or not. There are the beloved voices of our friends and family who tell us what *they* would want, despite the fact that we can't agree. There are the seductive voices of our fantasies that tell us what we'd *like* to want, although deep down we don't. And there is the devilishly loud voice of our own imp of the perverse that tells us to *deny* what we want, if only for the bittersweet hell of it.

Our dreams allow us to hear our inner voice through all the other voices. A friend of mine told me about a dream that performed this service for her when she was in the midst of refurbishing a newly purchased vacation house in upstate New York. She had been swamped with advice from professional and amateur decorators (including family members who'd be sharing the house), and she had meekly followed most of it; but there was one long, enclosed porch attached to the bedroom that she was determined to make her private domain and that she therefore wanted to decorate by herself. She tried out individual color swatches on the walls to no avail. Weeks went by, and she couldn't make up her mind what colors to use. All she did was attract lots of conflicting opinions from her hordes of advisors.

One night, she dreamed that she was a child again, about ten years old, visiting an ice cream parlor. She looked in all of the tubs of different flavors, but the instant she saw mint chocolate chip, she knew that she wanted it. She ran to her parents' home with her mint chocolate chip ice cream cone and entered a dark, deserted room she'd never seen before. She sat down in one corner of the room and began eating the ice cream cone with great pleasure. In front of her, through a long row of windows, she could see dark trees trembling in the wind. When she woke up, she knew that the dream room was her unpainted porch, which overlooked a woods; and she also knew that she wanted to paint the walls of the porch mint green with chocolate brown trim.

A member of my dream group who makes pottery once had a series of dreams that helped him reach a more complicated decision shortly after he graduated from college in Boston: whether to move to Seattle and join friends there who were forming an artists' colony or to move to New York, work independently, and pursue some leads he'd received from his teachers. It didn't help to draw up lists of pros and cons for either choice or to pool the responses of all his confidants. The two alternatives always wound up seeming equally desirable.

Finally, my dream group member reviewed all the dreams he'd had during that period about Seattle and/or New York. Tallying his experiences, he noticed that he'd felt much more dream anxiety in the Seattle environment than in the New York environment. Specifically, he'd been worried about getting along with his friends in Seattle and about being so far away from his other friends and contacts in Boston. This realization helped convince him to move to New York—a decision he might have reached in any event, but a decision he could formulate and accept with much more confidence, thanks to what his dreams showed him.

When it comes to making exceedingly tough decisions, it's vital to listen to our inner voices; and for this reason, dreams become all the more valuable as counselors. During my early months of research for this book, I participated in the home care of a twenty-year-old man with AIDS. Like all people who suffer from AIDS, he faced a bewildering number of manifestly life-or-death choices, particularly regarding his diet. Should he eat the way he'd always eaten before, so that his life would retain some comforting degree of normality? Should he eat all-natural foods, possibly only macrobiotic foods, to make his body healthier? Should he eat the foods he craved (such as the rich desserts so temptingly advertised on the TV set he had wound up watching most of the day), since the odds were so high that he had little time left to enjoy himself? Doctors, diet experts, and caretakers gave conflicting advice.

Late one afternoon, after tormenting himself over this issue, he fell asleep and had a dream in which his mother (who now lived in a distant state) came to his bedside wearing a beautiful nurse's outfit. She unrolled a chart and began talking about the basic food groups: fruits and vegetables, grains, dairy products, and meats.

In the context of the dream, the young man felt that he was listening to his mother rehearse a demonstration she was going to make as part of an audition for a new job, one that would enable her to live closer to him. When he awoke, however, the full import of the dream struck him: In his heart of hearts, he felt he should eat the basically sound, "three-square-meals" diet he'd always associated with health and home but had never taken seriously during his years on his own. The dream together with the dream-based decision making was very comforting to him—a clarion call to sanity under extremely distressing and confusing circumstances.

---

### Experiment: The Envelope, Please

The next time you have trouble making a choice among a number of equally plausible options, try invoking the help of your dreams. You can take either one, or both, of two basic approaches: keeping track of what your dream life tells you about your choices or incubating dreams to provide further enlightenment. Here is a combination strategy that is just weird enough, and yet psychologically cagey enough, to trigger a decision-making breakthrough:

1. Write out each choice—freely, without editing or rereading —on a separate sheet of paper. Then quickly tuck these sheets of paper into an envelope.

2. On another sheet of paper, write out a reward you will give to yourself once you reach your decision. Tuck that sheet of paper into the envelope and seal it.

3. Address the envelope to yourself and mail it.

4. Think about the envelope repeatedly while it is in the mail, and ask for a dream to answer it (*i.e.,* make a selection among the alternatives) by the time it arrives.

5. Write down any dream you remember, as soon as possible, during this period.

6. If the envelope arrives before you've recalled a dream that answers it, don't open it. Place it in a spot where you will

---

> see it easily and frequently each day and keep it there as a dream stimulant until you have a satisfactory dream answer.

## Picking Dreamflowers

The same process that applies to solving problems also applies to finding opportunities. In fact, most difficult situations that we confront present us with both problems and opportunities at the same time. Brainteasers in the academic world, for example, cause us intellectual pain and grief, but they can also make us smarter. If our house is crumbling all around us, we have the *problem* of repairing it, but we also have the *opportunity* of remodeling it into something we like better.

Problems throw our mental lives into flux, and in this flux, we're likely to imagine all sorts of new possibilities. Our dreams—which don't demand logic or thoroughness—provide a major forum for these possibilities to exhibit themselves. Therefore, when we have a dream that is clearly discussing a particular problem in our life, we need to examine it twice over. In addition to combing it for images that specifically suggest solutions to the problem, we need to keep an eye out for *any* novel and intriguing images that emerge. They may be clues leading us to see the positive aspects of a situation that our rational minds persist in labeling "negative."

Suppose you dream that a long-neglected acquaintance of yours brings you the solution to a nagging problem while the two of you are playing tennis. In addition to helping you solve your problem, your dream may inspire you to invite this person to try out a new tennis court with you, as a step toward rekindling a potentially advantageous relationship. If you glance longingly at a picture of a garden paradise during a dream about the trouble you're having at work, you may consider incorporating a walk through a local park into your daily schedule: not necessarily as a means of escaping your work problem, but as a means of enjoying life more wholeheartedly.

Above all, we need to form the habit of acting on our dreams, rather than simply thinking about them. One of the most difficult things to manage when we're experiencing a problem is the feeling that we're not in control of the situation—that because we lack any immediate solution, we're powerless to do anything. Dreams can offer us things to do, both to address the problem and to proceed with our lives during the time that the problem is disturbing us.

Whenever you wake up from a dream that you believe has been discussing a problem in your life, try to frame a resolution based on something that the dream has taught you. It might be a decision as cautious and general as "Listen to K— more closely, without interrupting" (something you didn't do in the dream, which aggravated matters); or it might be the first specific activity in a larger master plan, like "Check out schedules for adult education classes in Spanish" (a move in the direction that your dream indicated might strengthen your employment prospects).

As I mentioned previously, the artists of the language whom we label "romantic" tend to be the most persuasive in pleading the cause of dreams and dream-inspired gestures. Samuel Taylor Coleridge, who brought back visions of Xanadu from one of his dreams, made the following proposition: "What if in your sleep you dreamed, and what if in your dream you went to heaven and there plucked a strange and beautiful flower, and what if when you awoke you had the flower in your hand?" Coleridge's proposition has come true for many dreamers who have enhanced their everyday existence by pulling special images out of their dreams and into reality.

# 7

# Dreams and Creativity

OR THREE YEARS the French painter Saint-Pol-Roux shared a large, shabby Paris flat with several other artists. Whenever Saint-Pol-Roux wished to sleep, he hung a hand-carved sign on his bedroom door that guaranteed his friends wouldn't disturb him. It read, "Poet at Work." In April 1925, a drawing of that sign appeared in the controversial journal *La Révolution Surréaliste,* and the art world quickly adopted it as a symbol of the unique role played by dreams in the Surrealist aesthetic. In fact, we are all entitled to hang a "Poet at Work" sign on our bedroom door.

Regardless of whether we call ourselves artists when we're awake, we create wondrous dreams every time we sleep; and these dreams put us to mind-boggling work! They shock our senses, confound our logic, tease our expectations, and recast our memories. They can force us to navigate a runaway truck of leaky fuel oil down a dark mountain trail covered with red-hot golfballs. They can leave us naked in the punchbowl at Aunt Maggie's wedding reception. They can give us Godzilla as a babysitter.

Why are we dreampoets driven to cast ourselves in these bizarre situations? And why, in the light of day, should we take these bizarre dream adventures seriously? The answers to these questions lie in appreciating the link between dreams and creativity.

Like a poem, a painting, a garden, a game plan, or any other creative endeavor, a dream issues from a will to create that functions at the very core of the human psyche. Plato labeled this creative urge "the divine discontent." Other philosophers refer to it more positively as an individual's personal genius. All agree that since it is part of our human nature to feel confined, even deadened, by our rational understanding of things as they are, we goad ourselves to invent new arrangements. In no other context do we experience this spontaneous activity as consistently and forcefully as we do in dreams. If we dismiss our dreams, we not only forfeit a major share of our own creative productions, we also lose an excellent chance to study how our creativity operates, so that we can better recognize and develop creative impulses in our waking lives.

On those occasions when we succeed in expressing ourselves creatively, it is because we have bridged the gap between what is "true" to us and what is "real" in the world around us. When we dream, these bridges take the form of imaginary life scenes, charged with original details, patterns, and sensations. Often these scenes possess a refreshing, gamelike quality. In this respect, they are reminiscent of child's play, which psychologists claim is basically a self-generated educational process—a testing of possibilities. Consider this dream created by Alison Kroger, manager of a fitness center in Seattle and member of a biweekly dream group with five of her neighbors:

*I am carrying a wobbly rack filled with old, beat-up record albums across a recreation room in a dark basement. At first I move carefully, so the records won't spill from the rack. Then I realize I don't have to be careful because the records aren't really worth anything. So I fling the records all across the floor with great exuberance. I can't see where they've landed, and I wonder how I'm going to clean up the mess, but for the moment I still want to have fun. I start dancing around the room wildly. With every step, I land neatly on top of a record, and it begins to glow. I am amazed at how good the feeling is. When I stop dancing, I look back and I can see all the records softly glowing and in mint condition, lying on the floor of the room.*

Alison's dream stands on its own as a creative vision, but what particularly impressed her when she considered it later was the creation within the creation: the way her dream-self changed the records from "beat-up" to "mint condition." The dancing had been so much fun, and the image of the transformed records remained so mesmerizing, that she was inspired to fulfill the dream in her waking life. First she incorporated what she called a "fling" period into her own aerobics routine—a time at the end of her workout when she could move freely, following what felt good to her as she went along. Satisfied with how emotionally and physically exhila-rating the "fling" was, she added a similar period to the aerobics classes she conducted at her fitness center. She made only one alteration. In further tribute to her dream, she called the period "Minutes of Revolution."

A dream creation can be disturbing rather than refreshing. In such a case, we must appreciate that creativity is not necessarily synonymous with joy and beauty. Every creative act has an element of strangeness to it, a wild streak that demands our attention. We can easily become disoriented, annoyed, or downright threatened by the unfamiliar, even more so by the assertively unfamiliar. For this reason, we need to remind ourselves to be especially patient with dreams that are ugly or scary. Whether or not we like them, they can possess just as much creative benefit as pleasant dreams.

It was a horrendous nightmare in the spring of 1842 that in-spired Elias Howe to invent the sewing machine. Howe dreamed that a tribe of fierce cannibals abducted him from his home and bound him from head to foot. In exchange for his life, they de-manded a machine that could sew cloth. Unable to give them what they wanted, Howe was thrown into a large pot of water to be boiled alive. The last thing he remembered before he woke up trembling in his own sweat was the unusual spears the cannibals kept jabbing in front of his face: The point of each spear bore a sinister, eye-shaped hole. Haunted all day by this fearsome image, he suddenly realized that a sewing machine could work if the needle carried the thread at its tip. Chances are good that Howe would not have been sufficiently stirred to action by a milder dream image, say, a writing quill that had a hole in the nib. It was probably because the image of the spear was so unforgettably frightening that his mind kept working on it.

Some special dreams, such as the ones we have just examined, manage to trigger creative activities in the real world, but all dreams have their independent value as creative products and can give us valuable training toward more fully using our creative minds. Dreams break our routines, so that we can witness the unconventional. They give us new skills, or new scope for skills we already have, so that we can accomplish what might have seemed impossible. They breathe life into our hopes, fears, and intuitions, so that we can apprehend the intangible. They mix up cause and effect, so that we can increase our mental and emotional flexibility. Because specific dream images, sensations, and patterns represent the purest and most accessible products of our individual creative genius, they are especially promising sources of direct creative inspiration. Dreams also offer highly appropriate and effective raw material to use in exercises for developing creative thinking skills.

In general, techniques for achieving creative breakthroughs in waking life by working with dreams rely on one or more of the following procedures:

- We can make a deliberate effort to invest our waking life with the same spirit, energy, and metaphorical magic that we experience in our dreams.
- We can play with the images, sensations, and patterns in our dreams in order to gain proficiency in thinking creatively.
- We can produce creative works based on specific images,

sensations, and patterns in our dreams—both dreams that come to us spontaneously and dreams that we incubate for the express purpose of creative inspiration.

The experiments offered in this chapter will help you to master these techniques, so that you can attain whatever creativity goals you set for yourself.

## Setting Creativity Goals

A dream image does not have to be as intense as a mystically glowing disk or a menacing spear to instigate a real-life creative breakthrough. What makes the process work is the dreamer's readiness to see the creative potential of the image. The more involved we become in observing and nurturing creative growth in our daily lives, the more we can look to our nightly dreams to assist us.

The questions posed below ask you to recall incidents of creativity, or a lack of creativity, in your life history. You don't need to strain to produce answers. Simply pause after each question and allow memories and personal fantasies to surface in your mind, much as scenes appear in a dream.

The purpose of this exercise is to relive moments when creativity, or its absence, was a major issue, so that you can sharpen your ability to recognize personally meaningful "creative contexts" in the future, whether you encounter them in your waking life or in your dreams.

Some thunder-and-lightning experiences may be easy to remember: for example, a two-week period when you hammered out a daringly original business proposal that astonished your colleagues, or an ecstatic afternoon when you composed song after song on your neighbor's piano. More numerous and, therefore, more revealing in many respects are the creative efforts that are less dramatic and risk being overlooked in a speedy review: for example, a tricky, last-minute negotiation with a client when all the right things to say just popped into your mind, a time during a blizzard when you made a great-tasting meal out of the only five items left in the refrigerator, a festive occasion when you thought of the perfect gift to surprise your lover, or a summer when you made up ghost stories to entertain your four-year-old nephew.

Similarly, you may have no trouble recalling painful episodes in your life that made you cry out desperately for a creative solution: for example, a month-long, inexplicable slump in your work performance when you needed to be as sharp as you possibly could, the first year after a heartbreaking divorce when you didn't know what to do with yourself, or a hellish night at your class reunion when you were a tongue-tied idiot.

The more patiently and receptively you ponder your reactions to each of the questions below, the more mental images you will spawn, and the richer and more potent each image will be. These images will serve you well whenever you decide to incubate inspirational dreams or to review your dreams for creative ideas. Most important, they will help you to design specific creativity goals.

■ **What are some instances in your life when you have exercised creativity?**

After identifying a particular example, ask yourself: How did it happen? How did I feel during this period? Was there a series of different feelings involved? How did it affect my life and the lives of those around me? If I were to choose (or create) one clear image to symbolize this experience, what would it be?

■ **What are some instances in your life when you wish you had been more creative?**

After identifying a particular example, ask yourself: What prevented me from being creative? How did I feel during this period? Was there a series of different feelings involved? How did my lack of creativity affect my life and the lives of those around me? How might I have been more creative during this period? What might have occurred if I had been more creative? If I were to choose (or create) one image to symbolize this experience, what would it be?

- **What personal attributes make you creative, in your own estimation and in the estimation of other people?**

- **What circumstances in your environment stimulate your creativity?**

- **What personal attributes inhibit your creativity?**

- **What circumstances in your environment get in the way of your creativity?**

Now give separate consideration to each of the major areas of your life—your work, your home, your personal relationships, and your leisure time—and respond to these questions:

- **What are some ways in which you could be more creative in this area?**

- **What benefits might you gain by being more creative in this area?**

- **What might help you to become more creative in this area?**

- **What might prevent you from becoming more creative in this area?**

- **What might happen if you aren't more creative in this area?**

Establishing a detailed objective involving creativity is very challenging. Creativity is not something that can be expressed quantitatively. We can't plan for a project to be creative by rolling up our sleeves and computing numbers that will clarify exactly what resources we need, how much progress we're making along the way, and when we've finally achieved our desired outcome. What we *can* do is stay focused on images that will inspire us to be more creative.

For example, if you are an architect who wants to design an unorthodox office complex for a newspaper staff, you can visualize innovative buildings you have constructed in the past, or the logos and mastheads of newspapers you enjoy, or details you associate with newspapers, like editorial cartoons, green visors, computer screens, or press badges. The images that come to mind most clearly are liable to be the most promising catalysts for creativity. Assuming you are most intrigued by the image of columns of black and white print, you may discover that you can turn that image into a striking architectural feature, such as a colonnade of black and white pillars across the facade of the building.

Equally inspiring are the pictures we form to represent what we hope will happen as a result of our creative success (which can be envisioned as the final product itself or the reactions it might generate). Assuming you have the same objective of designing an office complex for a newspaper staff, you can imagine several unusual-looking shapes, colors, or textures filling the actual construction site, or an intriguing trophy presented to you for your work on the project, or a party set in a distinctive main lobby celebrating the opening of the building, or particular newspaper people thanking you for including specific features in the building. Any of these images may lead to a breakthrough idea for your project that is especially apt and ingenious.

Images that spark creativity are those that speak to us when we take a break from the business of waking life and simply listen. Many of these images present themselves in our dreams. Others spring forth while we're in the process of contemplating our dreams. And still others take shape when we regard life with a dreamlike frame of mind—which is perhaps the first step toward becoming a more creative human being.

## Turning Life into a Dream

Whether or not your dream life regularly supplies you with specific creative inspiration, it offers you a continuing illustration of the creative spirit at play. If you want to use your mind more creatively, the quickest, easiest, and most important thing you can learn from your dreams is the art of looking at your waking life in different, more imaginative ways.

A personal goal involving creativity may be as vague as "to get more pleasure out of my work" or "to put more romance into my love life." Essentially, realizing such a goal is a matter of changing your perspective on something and, accordingly, your behavior—a task you perform with ease every night in your dreams. It's the ability so often attributed to poets of transforming the ordinary (which can sometimes seem boring) into the newly mysterious, and the mysterious (which can sometimes seem spooky) into the comfortably ordinary.

It is well known that Franz Kafka worked with his dreams to create such twentieth-century literary masterpieces as *The Trial* and *The Castle*. It is not so well known that he also cultivated a creative, dreamlike mentality to make his administrative job at a workmen's compensation bureau more stimulating.

Kafka began shifting his perspective on life to a more creative one by forcing associations between images in his dreams and images in his job. A dream picture of a cliff pockmarked with vipers' nests became the rough draft of a contract, littered with inaccuracies. Later, he reversed the activity: He practiced recording what went on in his office in the same manner as he recorded what went on in his dreams, using the present tense and being careful to capture the magical singularity of each moment by respecting both its literal and its figurative nature. Instead of translating dream images into ordinary, waking-life terms, he was translating ordinary, waking-life images into the language of dreams.

In one creative diary entry, Kafka turned a telephone call he received at work from a nervous claimant into a strikingly dramatic and revealing dreamlike event:

*I am a king sitting on a throne. A black box screams near my right hand. I place part of it to my ear. A thin voice whispers against a howling wind—a voice of pain and fear. I see a forest of metal and a man stumbling through with a red leg. While the voice talks of the man, I take a bleeding twig and make symbols on a white square. I see the man walking confidently in the sunlight.*

In this diary entry, Kafka is a king—a man who has the power and authority to help his client; the screaming black box is his phone; the howling wind is the static on the phone; the forest of metal is the factory where Kafka's client has been injured, which Kafka visualizes as he hears about the accident; the bleeding twig is Kafka's pen; the symbols on a white square are words he writes on a sheet of paper; the man walking in the sunlight is Kafka's final mental image of the client, whom Kafka must now try to help. In rendering this imaginative version of what really happened, Kafka wound up communicating more about the incident's emotional, auditory, and visual impact on him than he could have communicated if he'd written about it in more objective, everyday terms.

Over the years, Kafka derived much satisfaction from what many of his peers considered a tedious occupation for a committed artist. His employers rewarded him with frequent raises and promotions, and he introduced new concepts in workplace safety that are credited with saving hundreds of lives in eastern Europe during the period between the world wars. In discussing Kafka's dream-influenced point of view, biographer Max Brod comments:

*To him, the office, including his own part in it, became as wonderful as a locomotive is to a small child. His attention to dreams kept his mind as alive and fertile as a child's. And it was this primordial awe of the mystery of things—of the miraculous and enigmatic inherent in every fact of what others took for granted—that was the source of his genius.*

---

## Experiment: Life Is But a Dream

In the spirit of Kafka, create dreamlike fantasy versions of different moments in your daily life. Use both routine and unusual occurrences as subject matter. For example, you may want to present a shopping trip as an epic quest in an alien universe or revise a troublesome confrontation at work into a wacky fairy tale with a hero and a villain. Try imagining vivid, full-blown scenarios for unexpressed emotions, fantasies, and flashes of insight you had during the day.

The object of your fantasy is to invest your waking experiences with as much wonder and unsettling originality as dream experiences typically possess. As a result, you will not only increase your general powers of creative expression, you will also be paying more specific attention to the world around you, how you really feel about what goes on in that world, and what possibilities there are for change.

---

## Turning Your Dreams into the News of the Day

Creativity begins with the capacity to grasp and articulate the possible meanings of an experience. Scientists call it the ability to generate abstract concepts from concrete sensations. Educators describe it as the skill of going from specific impressions to general ideas. Businesspeople refer to it as the talent for seeing the big picture in the little details. All three groups agree that achieving and keeping this mental agility entails systematic practice.

Dreams are especially good mediums for exercising mental agility because they are so fluid and multidimensional. Depending on your point of view, a single dream can look either serious or silly, instructive or entertaining, sophisticated or childlike, real or hallucinatory. To take advantage of the plastic quality of dreams, Tom Cowan, a freelance writer and founder in 1983 of the Brooklyn Dream Community, created an exercise in "dream-encapsulating" that he regularly conducts at dream-study workshops in the New York City area.

Cowan first asks participants to imagine one of their dreams is being reported in a newspaper or magazine and to give it an appropriate headline (or title) and one-paragraph summary. Then he encourages them to try out different journalistic styles, creating headlines and summaries for an article based on the dream that might appear in a relatively staid publication like *The New York Times*, a sensationalizing tabloid like *The National Enquirer*, and a special-interest periodical like *Psychology Today* or *Fashion Quarterly*.

Inevitably the meaning derived from the dream images changes with each reinterpretation, and yet the basic pattern of images remains the same. The result is a greatly increased chance of happening upon different "truths" that the dream contains. As Cowan says:

> *Most dreams display several meanings all at once. There are no "good" or "bad" titles. Any title, no matter how outlandish, will work if it has the power of conjuring up the details of the dream when you read it. The very process of creating different titles, selecting the images that you think are the most important with each title, paring off the details that seem secondary, and formulating the wording that says it best—all these mental activities prepare your conscious mind for seeing more deeply into the symbolic possibilities of the dream.*

The headline responses of "Gary," a man I met at one of the monthly Brooklyn Dream Community open houses, provide a straightforward example of how this exercise works. Here is Gary's dream:

> *I am with a group visiting an elaborate Gothic mansion in Louisiana that is now a museum. An elderly, bearded guide takes the group into a basement room that has a window revealing an underwater section of the Mississippi River. I bang on the glass and a beautiful mermaid appears. I try to hear what she's saying to me, but the guide is yelling at me about banging on the window.*

Here are Gary's headlines, designed for the four different publications mentioned above:

- *The New York Times:* Tourist Causes Disturbance at Southern Historical Site
- *The National Enquirer:* Mermaid Woos Man in Haunted House
- *Psychology Today:* Natural Wonders Can Trigger Hysterical Delusions
- *Fashion Quarterly:* Fresh Nautical Styles Draw Sharp Attack from Conservative Critics

Gary noted after the exercise that each title, together with its accompanying one-paragraph summary, gently directed his mind to a different "truth" about the dreams that might have gone undiscovered if he had restricted himself to one mood-of-the-morning explication. The *New York Times* headline, for example, caused him to realize that his private thoughts and fantasies (symbolized by the mermaid) might be distracting him from his "appointed rounds" at work (symbolized by the tour group). On the other hand, the *Fashion Quarterly* headline made him consider the "refreshing" value of acting on some of his more creative thoughts and fantasies, even though this might shock others around him.

It was fascinating for Gary to be able to identify different "truths" that lay embedded in that single dream. Even more exciting, however, was the liberating sense he experienced of flexing the same creative muscles he had used to produce the dream in the first place.

---

**Experiment: Read All About It!**

Follow Cowan's "dream-encapsulating" exercise with one of your own dreams: Imagine it is a real-life experience that you are recounting in a short newspaper or magazine story. Create titles and one-paragraph summaries to fit different types of publications. Use any publications you wish. You can even make up publications.

You can also perform a variation of this exercise developed by Frank Stefano, a tax consultant who, like Cowan, is also a Brooklyn resident and a longtime dreamworker. Imagine your dream is a movie and pick a title that would look good on a marquee—one that not only fits your dream but also is short, snappy, and intriguing enough to draw an audience off the street. Then write a capsule summary of the movie, like the ones that appear in newspaper or magazine reviews (Stefano particularly recommends *TV Guide* blurbs as models).

Repeat this same activity by turning your dream into different types of movies. Assuming, for example, that you had Gary's dream (described above) and originally imagined it as a light-hearted, adult, romantic fantasy movie, envision it instead as a children's movie, an espionage movie, a science fiction movie, a horror movie, a mystery, a documentary. Give each movie its own characteristic title and summary review. You may even want to cast it with celebrities, relatives, friends, or acquaintances, and determine suitable directors and shooting locales.

---

## Using Dream Material to Produce Visual Works of Art

You don't have to be a preliterate child, a habitual doodler, or a professional illustrator to appreciate how much easier it can be to express your emotions and ideas through pictures than through words. Verbalization involves mastering a well-defined and formal system of communication, while visualization evolves much more freely from our original sense impressions. We are not at all as likely to censor what we depict, either in our minds or on paper, as we are to censor what we put into words. No doubt this explains why dreams are so intensely visual, and why many of the most vociferous spokespeople for the inspirational power of dreams have been world-famous visual artists, including Michelangelo, El Greco, Goya, Gauguin, Picasso, Chagall, Dali, Klee, and O'Keeffe.

The more we strive to render images in our dreams into tangible works of art, the more vitally attuned we become to our own feelings. This integration can have an enormously beneficial effect both on our self-esteem as creative individuals and on the quality of our artistic productions. It's a matter of bringing our own authentic visions of the world into the light of day, where we can work on them and they can work on us.

Dr. Helene Fagin, a psychoanalyst based in Westchester County, New York, discovered the power of this connection during a special ten-month program she conducted for twelve women painters, sculptors, printmakers, and collage artists who lived and worked near her home. Practicing what Fagin had previously learned in an experiential dreamwork course taught by Dr. Montague Ullman, the twelve women met weekly to discuss their dreams, with special emphasis on any relationship that their dreams might have to their work.

As Fagin's program continued, each participant became increasingly more interested and adept in transferring dream images and moods into art projects. The resulting works were not only more personally satisfying, they were also more successful in the opinion of outside critics. Near the end of the program, one participant told Fagin:

*Yes, I may be doing the best work I've ever done. My paintings used to be so saccharine sweet. I never wanted anyone to know what went on in me. The dreams were allowing me to show other people what is really going on. The reviews have been phenomenal. One professor commented, "There seems to be a tremendous amount of growth." My sculpture teacher thought I was using my own struggle to show strong forms. The dream group opened up my feelings, delving into my metaphors, sometimes a little deeper than I wanted. The reception of these pieces has been interesting. Everyone sees the feelings in them and the dream images that I worked with. It is the first time that I have exhibited so many pieces together, actually set up a show with twenty pieces revealing my personality, exposing my guts.*

Whether or not you are accustomed to expressing yourself in the visual arts during your waking life, you do so each night in your dreams. One way to open a direct channel between your everyday self and your innate genius—a channel that can lead to creative breakthroughs in any type of real-world endeavor—is to devise visual images that replicate the experiences you have had in your dreams.

---

### Experiment: Night Visions

Draw a scene from a recent dream. Don't worry if the images in your drawing do not exactly correspond to the images in your dream. As long as you work with the same subject matter and strive to reproduce the same mood, your drawing will most likely evoke key elements of the dream world that inspired it.

If you are self-conscious about what you feel is a lack of drawing talent, try creating collages using pictures from old magazines. To make sure the collage reflects your dream, select pictures that portray the same subject matter and arrange them so that they convey a similar message or significance.

If a particular image in a recent dream stood out from all the others, focus on that image by itself and cast it into a work of art. As an alternative to a drawing or a collage, you can try creating a sculpture or montage based on dream material. A three-dimensional medium may be more appropriate for a dream

---

that had important tactile or architectural qualities or that featured a great deal of movement.

While you are working on your art project, keep your dream in mind. The dream will grow increasingly meaningful as you stay focused on recapturing it. To bring one of your dreams even more forcefully into your waking life, you may want to create an artwork with a practical purpose: a drawing that you can bestow on someone who appeared in the dream, an ornamental tool that you can use around the house, a graphic that can be printed on personal stationery.

## Using Dream Material to Produce Literary Works of Art

Dreams may be predominantly visual, and strong feelings may be more easily expressed in pictures than in words; nevertheless, many literary masterpieces were directly inspired by dreams, including Dante's epic *The Divine Comedy,* Voltaire's novella *Candide,* Coleridge's poem "Kubla Khan," Shelley's novel *Frankenstein,* Dostoyevsky's novel *Crime and Punishment,* Poe's poem "The Raven," Joyce's novel *Ulysses,* and Styron's novel *Sophie's Choice.* Great writers may be compelled to articulate their dreams precisely because those dreams are so nonverbal. We all depend on words to remember our dreams, and people gifted at literary expression may be irresistibly challenged to create a written portrait of a dream as richly textured and provocative as the dream itself.

Robert Louis Stevenson relied heavily on dreams to create many of his literary works. Tormented as a child by recurrent nightmares, Stevenson took the advice of his family physician and tried lulling himself to sleep by weaving pleasant stories in his mind. Almost immediately, his dream life became a source of entertainment rather than torment, even when specific images were disturbingly strange. He claimed that his entire career as a fiction writer grew out of this early storytelling therapy, and that many of his ideas were delivered to him in his sleep by what he termed his "little brownies." In his memoirs (where he frequently refers to himself in the third person), Stevenson boasts that whenever he feels pressured to write:

> ... at once the little people begin to bestir themselves in the same quest, and labour all night long, and all night long set before him truncheons of tales upon their lighted theatre. No fear of his being frightened now; the flying heart and the frozen scalp are things bygone; applause, growing interest, growing exultation in his own cleverness (for he takes all the credit), and at last a jubilant leap to wakefulness, with the cry, "I have it, that'll do!" upon his lips.

The best-known production of Stevenson's "brownies" is *The Strange Case of Dr. Jekyll and Mr. Hyde*, a work that appropriately centers on the struggle between the rational, daytime self and the irrational nighttime self. Describing the genesis of his creation, Stevenson wrote:

> I had long been trying to write a story on this subject, to find a body, a vehicle, for that strong sense of man's double which must at times come in upon and overwhelm the mind of every thinking creature.... Then came one of those financial fluctuations.... For two days I went about racking my brains for a plot of any sort; and on the second night I dreamed the scene at the window, and a scene afterwards split in two, in which Hyde, pursued for some crime, took the powder and underwent the change in the presence of his pursuers.

In the decades since Stevenson made this admission, writers have been much more consciously involved in linking their external creations to their internal creations. Jack Kerouac often told interviewers that a major part of his "writing ritual" was mining his dream journal for scenes, phrases, and self-made words he could incorporate in his narratives. When critics attributed his revolutionary prose rhythms to his enthusiasm for jazz, Kerouac agreed, but added that an equally important influence was the loose-limbed style he developed in his dream journal to tag down fleeting dream impressions.

Graham Greene, a decidedly more traditional stylist, also derives plot ideas for his novels from his dreams. During a seminar at Georgetown University in October 1986, he insisted:

> A major character has to come somehow out of the unconscious. I cata-logue my dreams, searching for the tracks of a fresh character. Because I was psychoanalyzed when I was 16, I have always been interested in dreams and the unconscious.

Padgett Powell, a young novelist just beginning to attract favorable critical attention, is similarly indebted to dreams. His latest book, *A Woman Named Drown,* heralded in *The New York Times Book Review* as "a potent, funny, one-of-a-kind sort of book," was based on a dream the author had several years ago while attending a writing workshop at the University of Houston. Powell admits that he felt a bit silly at first about being so preoccupied with the dream, but he was unable to forget it or to shake the feeling that it could be developed into a singularly powerful work of art. Fortunately for his readers, he followed his dream.

Twentieth-century poets have been just as susceptible to the exotic imagery and structure of dreams as their novelist counterparts. Sylvia Plath, Adrienne Rich, W. S. Merwin, James Dickey, and Robert Bly are among the more famous poets who have produced works they have identified as virtual dream transcripts.

Lyricists, too, have depended on their dreams for fresh ideas. The rock star Sting, for example, has been a faithful recorder of his dreams since adolescence. In 1985, he told a *Newsweek* reporter:

> The line *"every breath you take"* [the title of an enormously success-ful 1983 recording by Sting's group, Police] *came to me in a dream. So did the concept and words for "The Dream of the Blue Turtles"* [Sting's first hit solo album in 1985]. *I dreamed that four gigantic*

> *turtles crashed through my garden wall and began tearing up the lawns and flower beds. These massive, macho, virile, prehistoric blue turtles were rolling around, doing back flips, wrecking everything. I decided that these creatures ruining my tidy garden were the four musicians I had just hired in order to take an entirely different musical direction.*

The nineteenth-century writer Jean-Paul Richter prefigured the twentieth-century painter Saint-Pol-Roux when he stated, "A dream is an involuntary kind of poetry." Dreams are a rich source of creative images, and the effort to translate them is a rich source of creative growth. By *voluntarily* forging our dreams into literary works, we learn to stretch our language skills and, in the process, our capacity to communicate more creatively both to ourselves and to others.

## Experiment: A Write to Know

Take images or scenes from a recent dream and use them as the basis for a short story, a poem, or a song lyric. Your literary work can be as brief as a one-paragraph fable or a two-line stanza, providing it has a narrative structure. Typically, a narrative structure consists of three major parts: a beginning (the "setting," which establishes some sort of conflict), a middle (the "action," which develops that conflict), and an ending (the "resolution," which brings the conflict to a "logical" conclusion).

Many dreams (at least, dreams that we remember well) have a built-in tripartite narrative structure, so you may not need to work very hard to organize your material. If you choose to work with a dream fragment, say, a solitary image that is particularly striking, then improvise a story that makes sense of that fragment and gives it a central role in some sort of drama.

Try casting the same dream, or dream images, into different literary formats, such as a fairy tale, a nursery rhyme, a haiku, a horror story, a travelogue, a ballad, a memoir, a written confession, a jingle, a play, a letter, an account of an ancient myth. You may find that one particular format reveals depths of meaning that other formats don't. Or you may find that your work with the dream in one particular format produces a more exciting and personally satisfying work of art.

You can also play around with different literary styles. Pick a writer you like who has a distinctive voice (for example, Charles Dickens, Agatha Christie, Mickey Spillane, Gertrude Stein, Dr. Seuss, Bob Dylan) and render your dream into words as this writer might have expressed it in one of his or her works. If you can think of a writer, or a specific literary work, that particularly suits the tone or subject matter of your dream, this endeavor can be all the more fun and illuminating. Like any exercise in imitation having to do with the arts, the purpose of this activity is to practice different ways of expressing your dream. You may hit on a mode of expression that is especially meaningful or intriguing. The essence of creativity is such a fortunate discovery.

## Applying Specific Dream Material to Life/ Work Projects

Being creative does not necessarily mean being artistic. It means putting our personal insights into action, no matter what the arena may be. The process begins with recognizing a creative idea when we have one. Above all, a creative idea seems fresh to us. We can feel it take shape in our own minds, alongside, but separate from, the ideas that we borrow ready-made from other sources, or that we put together mechanically using logic and the data at hand. A creative idea points to possibilities that may not be new from a cosmic point of view, but that are definitely new to us. If we cultivate that idea and help it to take shape in our lives, then we are being creative—just as we are with our dream productions each night.

Unfortunately, our immediate reaction to creative ideas is the same as our immediate reaction to dreams: We reject them because of their strangeness. They don't fit into our habitual frame of reference, so we consider them worthless at best and counterproductive at worst.

Granting people the time and space to accept their dreams as sources of creative ideas has been the ten-year mission of Mark Seidler, cochairperson of Cerebrics, a management consulting firm specializing in corporate creativity seminars. Recently, Seidler conducted a weekend, off-site program for ten executives of a computer software firm. Two months after the program was over, one of the participants wrote to Seidler:

> *While I enjoyed it* [the program], *I'll have to confess that I didn't think it would have any significant impact on my future work. Then, several weeks ago, I had a dream where I walked all around my department and observed people at work. It was very busy, people wouldn't even stop their work to notice me, but it was absolutely quiet. No phones ringing, no chatter in the halls, no noisy deliveries. At first the dream bothered me. I felt as if I'd been deaf. But as you advised, I held on to the dream and kept thinking about it. Finally I realized how peaceful that quietness had been, and I connected that peacefulness with how much work had been getting accomplished.*
>
> *Now I have instituted a "quiet hour" in my department. During the first hour in the morning, no calls are received (except by the switchboard), no appointments are set up for outsiders, and no interoffice visits are made. Instead, people can work undisturbed at their desks. The reaction has been wonderful. People are now asking me if we can add another "quiet hour" to the schedule!*

Some people are naturally good at recognizing a dream opportunity when it presents itself. Early in 1987, ten-year-old Claudine Rad of New York City had a beautiful dream featuring six fruit trees in a field of grass. Each tree exuded a distinct fragrance—banana, cherry, orange, lemon, coconut, and strawberry—and even the grass had a delightful, minty scent. Her mother, Nahia, was so impressed when she heard about the dream that she was determined to make it come true. Together with her daughter, she created a line of natural perfumes for children called "Whiffy Wear." It premiered in June at an exhibit in Macy's, where it kindled such excitement that the Rads are now shipping it to commercial outlets throughout the eastern United States.

Dreams speak about all facets of life, and they have inspired all manner of creative life/work projects, from the monumental and exalted, such as Gandhi's "hortal" or "passive strike" campaign in India, to the mundane and ephemeral, such as the title for the popular 1960s television show "Bonanza." To ignore your dreams is, in many respects, to turn your back on your own private oracle.

---

## Experiment: A Correspondence Course

Take an unusual image from a recent dream and look for corresponding images in the real world, both near-matches and images that have only one or two features in common with your dream image.

If, for example, you dreamed of a burning shoe, compare it to the shoes in your closet and shoes you've recently observed on other people, in stores, in periodicals, in TV shows, or in the movies. Consider items that are shaped like a shoe, or serve the same function as a shoe, or are made from the same materials as a shoe, or that have the sound "shoe" in their name. Also consider the many connotations of "burning" and then determine what "burning" might imply for each of the corresponding images you have identified.

After you have experimented with different images from dreams, go through this same process with different activities, patterns, and complete scenes from dreams.

The purpose of this analysis is to surround your dream visions with a wealth of associations from your waking world, so that you can increase your chances of hitting upon a creative insight.

Another, more focused way to generate correspondences be-

---

tween your dream material and your waking world is to imagine that your dream is a commercial for a product or service that doesn't yet exist. What might this product or service be? Then imagine that your dream is a public service message regarding some as yet unrealized aspect of your life or work. To what might this message refer? Bear in mind that commercials and public service messages can take the form of warnings as well as promotions.

## Dreaming with Open Eyes

To the person interested in becoming more creative, it is not so much what dreams *mean* that is important, but what dreams *do*. They show us new worlds. They give us new sensations. They suggest new arrangements. These dream adventures are wasted on us, however, if we don't equip ourselves in advance to be intelligent and responsive travelers. As Arthur Koestler said in his seminal book, *The Act of Creation,* "Creative inspiration never comes out of the blue; like grace, it comes only to the prepared mind which has already gathered together a whole host of relevant facts, impressions, and ideas."

In order to turn a dream into a work of art or a creative life/work project, you first need to condition yourself to look at the real world creatively, with the eyes of a dreamer. What would you like to see changed? What do you fear might happen? What are the possible ramifications of a given event? What invests particular objects you encounter with a special charm that similar objects don't have? Why do certain people intrigue you more than others? Develop the habit of asking yourself questions that you don't usually ask, and answering questions that you usually avoid answering. Then go on to practice some of the creativity experiments recommended in this chapter.

The final step toward becoming a more creative dreamer is to intentionally bring your hopes, fears, and wonders to bed with you.

Right before you fall asleep, try meditating on a particular creative goal you wish to achieve, or on a mystery that is stimulating your creative interest, or on some aspect of your life or work that you wish to revitalize by exercising creativity. Tell yourself that you will dream creatively on this subject and, the next morning, note any dream material that strikes you as remarkable, whether or not it appears to relate to your previous meditation.

The results of dream incubation can be particularly exciting and creatively empowering, as evidenced by some of the examples I mentioned in Chapter Six, "Dreams and Problem Solving." It's important to keep in mind, however, that dream incubation works very subtly. It may take lots of practice—both in trying to incubate a dream and in doing dreamwork on your incubated dreams—before you establish an identifiable "hit": a dream image that represents a clear and satisfying response to your incubation.

Above all, dream incubation is something you should experiment with—not something you should count on or worry about. In fact, if you *strain* to incubate a dream, you most likely will be working against yourself. By spending so much effort *insisting* that you dream about a particular subject, you may be using up all the psychic energy that your mind has for dealing with the subject. In such a case, your dreams may shift to some other aspect of your life. You can also become so single-minded about what you *want* your dreams to be saying that you overlook what they truly *are* saying when you perform your subsequent dreamwork.

Dream incubation involves the easy and enjoyable procedure of making a wish. As we learn in childhood through the wisdom of myths and folktales, and as we learn in adulthood from actual case histories, our wishes can bring us dreams and our dreams can help make our wishes come true. Certainly many creative artists deliberately look to their dreams for creative inspiration. The fact that from time to time they wind up getting inspiration from their dreams owes a lot to their predisposition to expect inspiration from their dreams. This expectation is at the heart of dream incubation. The rest is a matter of attaching some specific images—images associated with creativity goals—to this fundamental expectation. Then, simply sleep on it and see what happens.

That there is a link between dreams and creativity is impossible for anyone who has seriously looked at dreams to dispute. That creative people have devised many ways to work with dreams to enhance their personal creativity is understandable, given their own creative impulses as well as the creative nature of dreams. Nevertheless, the single most effective way to bring more creativity into your life through dreams is as simple, fun, and instructive as child's play: Stay mindful of the dream images that impress you, so that one day they may reward you. To paraphrase Socrates, the unexamined dream life isn't worth living.

# 8

# *Further* *Dream* *Adventures*

O<small>N</small> J<small>UNE</small> 14, 1986, I flew over Leningrad. The day was spectacularly clear and sunny. Light flashed off the chrome of bug-sized automobiles, gold cupolas burned with molten intensity, and the dark river Neva, stretching beneath me, glimmered like a jeweled belt. As I approached the Peter and Paul Fortress, I strained my eyes to catch a glimpse of the inner courtyard. There stood a crowd of people wearing scarlet robes, their faces turned upward, and in the center of the crowd, a ring of fur-clad strong men clutching a big circle of canvas. I shifted the angle of my outspread arms and veered toward the canvas. Looking down, I could see my shadow gliding slowly across the blue-gray roof of the fortress, head bobbing slightly and pants flickering in the wind.

The entry in my 1986 journal that records this dream offers no discussion of what it might mean in terms of my waking life, and frankly, that aspect doesn't interest me. Some experts (notably Freud) claim that flying dreams represent a desire for sexual release. Other experts interpret a flying dream as a wish to escape a bad situation or to transcend one's limitations. There are even experts who invoke the tongue-twisting rule "ontogeny recapitulates phylogeny" to explain flying dreams: Since stages in our prenatal development hark back through evolution to the birds, they argue, we may be born with a subconscious predisposition to realize our innate flying potential in our dreams.

Any or all of these theories may be true, but what really interests me about flying dreams is the fun factor. I think that we probably take to the air in our dreams because it's an exciting thing to do, and that this quality in itself gives such dreams their most significant meaning. Feeling this way, I'm more inclined to savor flight dreams as experiences unto themselves than to analyze them as symbolic representations of other experiences. After reviewing several months of dream entries, I usually look at all the flying dreams separately and admire each one as I would a cherished art object or a special memory.

Most of us have flight dreams from time to time and can attest that they are almost always exhilarating dreams. Published research papers, dream journals, and dreamwork accounts show that flying patterns can vary greatly and delightfully from dream to dream— as well as from individual to individual. Ann Sayre Wiseman, a writer in Cambridge, Massachusetts, who is now compiling a book devoted to flying dreams, distinguishes these major patterns of movement (among others): flapping, floating, swimming, long-distance leaping, shooting (like a cannonball), soaring (either birdfashion or Superman-fashion), riding air channels, levitating, and what she calls "assist flying" (air travel made possible by means of a device such as a magic stick, carpet, or chair). Different flight dreams also attempt different heights, velocities, durations, acrobatic maneuvers, and supplementary in-flight activities.

That flight dreams are so widespread, playful, and various suggests that dreams have a recreational value apart from their ability to help us achieve specific, waking-life goals. The same truth applies to dreamwork. Both activities can be worthy and rewarding exploits in their own right, allowing us to enjoy ourselves in all sorts of unique ways.

This chapter discusses several major methods of attaining one general goal that every dreamer can support—making dreams and dreamwork more pleasurable and adventurous. Part of the chapter deals with the private pleasure and adventure we can derive as a result of cultivating a particular kind of dreaming experience, such as lucid dreaming or waking dreaming. Another part of the chapter deals with the public pleasure and adventure that we can generate through sharing our dreams with other dreamers, from individuals who already have an intimate role in our lives to whole groups of people who are relative strangers.

Before I talk about sources of pleasure in the world of dreams, however, I'd like to address a major source of pain in the world of dreams: the nightmare. Although a nightmare certainly qualifies as an adventure, it's an adventure that can trouble us to the point where we fear to dream at all. The first step in deriving more pleasure from our dreams is to address any such fear and put it into proportion. There are many ways we can eventually master our nightmares and fly off into the sunrise.

## Taming the Nightmare

The flip side of excitement is fear. Unfortunately, fear generally has a stronger emotional impact. If flying dreams can start the heart beating louder and the adrenaline pumping faster, so can night-mares—so much so that they jerk us out of our slumbers far more often and linger in our memories a great deal more forcefully than their positive counterparts.

Nightmares have such frightening power because they connect us with fears that date from our childhood: fears we may have learned to put aside as we matured, but fears that never entirely went away. Our childhood fear of falling, for example, may re-emerge in a dream as a terrifying stumble over a cliff or a car ride off the side of a bridge. A dream in which our feet turn to lead as we try to escape an enemy may revive our long-forgotten frustration over a lack of muscle coordination or speed. We may once again, thanks to our dreams, be scared by fire, sharp objects, dark places, or beings larger than ourselves that we don't understand. We may also suffer wholeheartedly, as we did in our infancy, over a possible or actual lack of support from our loved ones.

All of these primal fears remain beyond the scope of reason to banish entirely because they came *before* reason in our emotional and mental development, at a time when we were vastly more impressionable. Whenever we feel vulnerable, small, powerless, or insignificant as adults, our dreams may automatically tap these deep-rooted, prerational feelings. Scratch any nightmare and you'll most likely find an image from a childlike world.

Even adult hero figures never completely outgrow the frights and phobias of their earliest years. Mickey Mantle was thirty-seven years old when he left baseball in 1967, and immediately he started having recurrent nightmares about his change in status. The first series of nightmares would always begin with him standing outside Yankee Stadium, dressed in his uniform, late for a game. As he tells it:

> *I could hear them saying, "Now batting, No. 7, Mickey Mantle," and I'd try to crawl through a hole into Yankee Stadium and I'd always get stuck. Looking through the hole, I could see Casey Stengel and Whitey Ford and all them out there and I couldn't get in. And I'd wake up and I'd be sweating like hell. I had that dream a long time.*

Even now, Mantle admits that he still has nightmares about no longer playing baseball:

> *I dream like I'm trying to pinch hit and I can't, I just can't hit, and if I do hit the ball, I can't get to first. I don't even know the guys I'm playing. But I know one thing: They keep waiting for me to hit one out,*

*and I never do. I'm thinking, "Jeez, I could at least hit* one *here," and everybody's saying, "He's really gonna hit one in a minute, boy!" And then*—*phtt*—*I pop up or something. (both quotes from Steven Erlanger, "In Search of Toots Shor: Mantle's Back,"* The New York Times, *February 5, 1988, p. B2)*

The plot of Mantle's nightmare may have changed, but the aura of childhood still persists. Any kid can relate to the fear of being athletically incompetent, disgraced in front of strangers, unable to live up to expectations, as well as the fear of being banished, held back, stuck in a hole. And any adult who has nightmares can recite similar, equally childlike horror stories.

Recurrent nightmares are common, not only because we each tend to develop our own limited set of especially frightening images, but also because the simple repetitiveness of an image can, in itself, express a fear of being trapped or having no alternative. It's also common to experience numerous nightmares over the course of a year, as we go through up-and-down emotional cycles.

What remains undefined by experts is whether an individual should be concerned about the *frequency* of his or her nightmares. In other words, how much is too much?

There is no answer to this question. It's entirely a subjective decision, based partially on how one defines "nightmare." Nevertheless, there are some guidelines for determining whether you're getting more than the average share, and if so, whether it's to be expected, given your general psychological makeup.

Dr. Ernest Hartmann, director of the Sleep Research Laboratory of the West-Ros-Park Mental Health Center at Lemuel Shattuck Hospital in Boston, estimates that only about one in two hundred people has nightmares every week. He also claims that certain dreamers are naturally disposed to endure more nightmares, or more shattering nightmares, than other dreamers. He refers to these people as having "thin boundaries." In describing them, he notes:

*They don't keep things pigeonholed. As a child grows up, he learns to distinguish between himself and others, between fantasy and reality, between dreaming and waking. These boundaries can be thin and fluid or thick and rigid. When a person has thin interpersonal boundaries, he tends to get easily involved, perhaps overwhelmed, in relationships. Then there are waking versus sleeping boundaries. Some of us wake immediately, but those with thin boundaries may take as many as 30 minutes before they're fully conscious of being awake. In matters of sexual identity, a person with thick boundaries says, in effect, "I am a man (or woman), and men do things this way." He's not in doubt. A thin-boundaries person is usually not overtly bisexual, but he might have more sexually ambiguous fantasies. (from Susan Seliger, "In the Dead of Night, Warns a Student of Nightmares, Childhood Fears May Shatter Sweet Dreams,"* People, *March 11, 1985, p. 128)*

Hartmann believes that thin-boundary people are more likely to have frequent or intense nightmares because they don't possess the strong defenses that other people have. They permit scary material into their dreams that others keep out. In advancing this theory, Hartmann does not mean to label thin boundaries as negative in general. He suggests that thin boundaries can also be responsible for especially liberating dreams, not to mention acts of unusual compassion and sensitivity in waking life. What he does intend is to make people aware of a possible explanation for their nightmares, so that they can receive and treat them with greater understanding.

Whether we have thick, thin, or medium boundaries, there are ways we can reduce the impact of virtually all our nightmares, rid ourselves of certain kinds of nightmares, or even turn specific nightmares into triumphs. The most important step toward any of these goals is to make a point of recording and studying our nightmares regularly. This will enable us to recognize possible waking-life triggers of our nightmares — current situations that are causing us to feel anxious, helpless, or lost, or that remind us of some period in our past (particularly in our childhood) when we felt similar emotions. Keeping watch over our dreams will also give us a clearer picture of our relative strengths and weaknesses, psychologically, emotionally, mentally, and even physically. All of this information will help us to cope with our lives in a more self-aware and constructive manner, so that we're not so susceptible to a nightmare "reflex." Our dreams won't have to attack us quite so fiercely to get us to face what's bothering us.

Additional procedures for nightmare management vary slightly according to the situation. Strong, recurrent nightmares can be so disruptive to one's sleeping pattern that some sort of professional therapeutic intervention is advisable. Most individual and recurrent nightmares, however, can be tamed by following these steps on a case-by-case basis:

1. Define as precisely as possible all the feelings you went through during the nightmare and its immediate aftermath. It's preferable to do this right after you awake from the nightmare, while lying still and silent in bed, but if you don't do it then, do it later the same day.

   Ask yourself questions that will pin down exactly what emotions were involved: Were you afraid of being injured, attacked, exposed, humiliated, betrayed, incriminated, robbed, rejected? When you woke up, did you feel hopeless, frustrated, terrified, angry, sorrowful, ashamed, grief-stricken, worthless?

   The more articulate you can be about what happened to you emotionally, the more rational you can be about overcoming or forestalling this kind of nightmare (not to mention its waking-life equivalent) in the future.

2. Think of everything you could have done in the dream to make it end more positively. Be sure to consider all things possible in the wide world of dreaming. For example, if you found yourself being assaulted by a monster, you might have taken any of these actions: fighting back and winning, talking the monster out of bothering you, kissing the monster and turning it into a wonderful human being, reducing the monster to a minuscule size

and blowing it away, enlarging yourself to a gigantic size and blowing it away, flying away from the monster altogether, and so on.

3. Decide which of the above strategies you'll use if the monster ever bothers you again. (If you're still in bed after waking up from the nightmare, try resuming sleep, with the confident intention not to go through the same experience again.) In later sleep, you may wind up replaying the nightmare with a positive ending, or you may have banished the nightmare forever, simply by working through it in your conscious mind.

4. In the case of an especially troubling or frequently recurring nightmare, write down the plot of the nightmare, the emotions you felt during as well as after the nightmare, and alternative happy endings for the nightmare. Then write a revised plot, based on the ending you like best. Read this revised plot several times and then replay it in your mind, as if you were performing a visualization exercise. Repeat this activity several times during the day following the nightmare, and as often as you feel is necessary (or pleasurable) thereafter.

5. Try sharing the nightmare with someone you trust. Often, nightmares are outlets for feelings that don't get expressed any other way; and if you unburden yourself to a friend or family member through dream sharing, you may release the tension that caused the nightmare. The same purpose may be accomplished by turning the subject matter of the nightmare into a work of art, such as a painting, a poem, or a short story. (Since a nightmare tends to be based on childhood fears, a related narrative that reads "safely" like a children's story may be the most successful exorcising artwork of all.)

Besides managing our own nightmares, many of us are called upon to help children deal with their nightmares, which, for reasons we've already examined, are typically more frequent and more intense than the nightmares of adults. As a rule, nightmares are most noticeably troublesome to children between the ages of three and five, when they are just beginning to develop self-consciousness and to take an active role in forming their social personalities. It is a period when they are acutely sensitive to their own needs and limitations and, therefore, mentally and emotionally preoccupied with every possible threat to their well-being.

Nightmares may also plague children from birth to three years old, but since they can't let us know much about them during those nonverbal years, we can't do much about them. If children are still having frequent nightmares as they approach adolescence, adult guardians may have grounds for serious concern. According to Hartmann, "There may be a heightened risk of suicide. They may need therapy or they may just need a friend, to have someone pay more attention to them."

While children are under ten years old, however, the frequent occurrence of nightmares is typically not a danger signal but a normal and healthy part of growing up. Nevertheless, every nightmare is a serious proposition in itself; and there are things you can and should do to assist a child to cope with his or her nightmares more effectively.

The most important thing to remember is to respond to a child's nightmare-related fears in a calm, reassuring, and above all, *reasonable* manner. For instance, if a child is scared to go to sleep at night because he or she might have a nightmare, it's a good idea to leave the bedroom door ajar or to turn on a soothing radio station or night light. Otherwise, a harmful syndrome of sleeplessness or shallow sleep might develop.

Resorting to fantasy games, such as pretending to eradicate the cause or effect of the nightmare with magic or derring-do, may only aggravate the problem. Dr. Carolyn Schroeder, a pediatric psychologist at the University of North Carolina, cites a bad example of this kind of nightmare mismanagement from her own professional experience:

*A child repeatedly woke up screaming about a bear in the closet. The father's response was to rush into the room offering to shoot the bear. But so far as the child was concerned, this did nothing to prevent the bear from returning the next night and the night after that. The father would have had much more success turning on a light and showing the child that there was no bear in the closet.*

It is also never wise to belittle the nightmare victim's anxiety or to dismiss the nightmare as foolish. Dr. John E. Mack, professor of psychiatry at Harvard Medical School, remarks:

*There's no point telling him* [the nightmare victim] *his dream is not real, because he had a very real nightmare. The important thing is to explain that there was never really any danger that* [images in the dream itself] *could possibly harm him.*

Other procedures to consider when helping a child adjust to a specific nightmare are:

- Encourage the child to talk about what happened in the nightmare. It's not necessary (and in most cases not advisable) to comment or pass judgment on what the child tells you. The important thing is to help the child to calm down through "talking it out." As a side benefit, you can gain some clues regarding the underlying causes of the nightmare, but it's best to keep such thoughts to yourself, so that the child can reach his or her own, unprejudiced understanding of what the nightmare means.

- Ask the child to describe what he or she could do the next time (that is, if the nightmare ever comes again) to make things better. This technique will prompt the child to rehearse coping strategies, both consciously and subconsciously, not only for this specific nightmare but for other similar dream-life or waking-life situations.

■ Ask the child to draw a picture of what scared him or her. Once a child externalizes the image in this way, it becomes far less threatening.

■ Take the advice of Dr. Robert Van de Castle and explain to the child that dreaming is like watching television. "You can say that most of the programs playing in your head are lots of fun," he counsels, "but if you're scared by what you see, you can always change the channel."

In addition to nightmares, children are also subject to "night terrors," which are commonly confused with nightmares but are actually very different. From the time one of my godchildren was an infant until he was over four years old, he suffered a night terror about every six months, a pattern which is perfectly normal, according to medical experts. He would wake up screaming and, sometimes, cry out for his parents, but when they came to his bedside, he would almost always resist their efforts to comfort him. Sometimes, he'd even scream louder, as if his parents themselves were antagonizing him. A specific episode might last as long as a half hour before he would fall back asleep; and the next morning, he could never recall being scared.

What all of my godson's caretakers soon learned is that night terrors are not caused by scary images. In fact, they are not dreams at all. When my godson appeared to wake up, he was actually still in a very deep stage of sleep, even though his eyes were open. Twice he literally awoke in the midst of his screaming; but he could only articulate vague causes for his panic—"I can't breathe" in one case and "Something hit me" in the other—and both times, he failed to recollect the experience when he showed up for breakfast.

No one knows for sure what makes the night-terror victim suddenly scream (and, in some cases, thrash about, sit up, or even sleepwalk), but the most likely catalyst is a sudden pain or physical discomfort that is more surprising than serious to the sleeper. Dr.

Richard Ferber of Children's Hospital in Boston recommends not worrying about a child's night terrors unless any flailing around during the experience itself threatens to injure the child:

> *Since the child is usually asleep throughout the whole episode, talking to him about it at the time is worthless. When he's awake, he won't remember what scared him so he doesn't need your help. Questioning him the next morning about what happened may only make him more anxious.*

Usually, night terrors disappear once a child reaches school age; however, it is not uncommon for older children, adolescents, and even adults to have night terrors on rare occasions. The characteristics that distinguish them from nightmares remain the same, regardless of the age of the sleeper: a panicky physical reaction (such as thrashing, sweating, or screaming), a continuation of the deep-sleep state (in most cases), and no detailed imagery of the type associated with dreaming. Although night terrors are momentarily shocking, they are seldom symptomatic of any major psychological or physiological problem, and they don't have any lingering after-effects.

## Lucid Dreaming

Every so often, most of us experience the sensation of being conscious that we are dreaming *while* we are dreaming. Usually, an especially odd image tips us off. We reach down to pick up a penny and our hand drifts painlessly through the floor. We look up from our newspaper on a train and notice that we're slithering across the ocean floor. We try to walk through a doorway and we can't, because our antlers are too wide. At such moments, we say to ourselves, "I must be dreaming!" And that's about as long as the sensation lasts. We either continue dreaming without being aware of it, or we wake up altogether.

In recent years, however, dream researchers have given new

meaning to this freak form of dual consciousness. They have learned how to encourage it and extend it, to the point where the dreamer can actually exercise conscious control over the content of his or her dream as it goes along. Known as "lucid dreaming," it's a form of creative consciousness that has astounding potential for self-amusement, not to mention self-development.

At the forefront of the lucid dreaming revolution is Stanford University's Dr. Stephen LaBerge, a dream scholar who was truly in the right place at the right time. In 1970, LaBerge was studying expanded mental states connected with Eastern spirituality, which led him one evening to attend a lecture by a Tibetan Buddhist master, who spoke of the art of "awakening in a dream." Later that same night, LaBerge had the following dream:

> *I was climbing K2 in the Himalayas, the second highest mountain in the world. The wind was whistling in my ears and the snow was drifting all around me. I happened to look down at my arm and noticed it was bare. "What's this?" I asked. "With only a T-shirt on, I'll freeze to death!" Suddenly I understood—I was dreaming. So I raised my arms, jumped in the air and flew away. (from Anne Fadiman, "American Dreamer," Life, November 1986)*

LaBerge's dream recalled a series of undersea adventure dreams he'd been able to create for himself, night after night, when he was six years old. Emboldened by this reminder of what he'd accomplished spontaneously as a child, he began experimenting to see if he could induce a lucid dream and then direct the course of the dream according to his wishes. He found he could do this fairly often simply by psyching up the night before, so he set a more ambitious professional goal: to *prove* that he was controlling his dreams and thereby establish lucid dreaming as a scientific fact.

LaBerge achieved his goal with two different laboratory demonstrations. The first one involved the prearrangement of an up-and-down eye signal that LaBerge was supposed to give to communicate that he was lucid during a dream. Before he retired for the night, he connected himself to a polygraph that would measure his eye movements and brain waves, and seven hours later, he became conscious in his dream body as he dreamed he was reading an instruction booklet for a vacuum cleaner. Right away, he started moving his dream finger up and down in front of his eyes. His eyes followed his finger, and the recording pens on the polygraph registered the telltale movement for all the lab technicians to see.

Despite numerous successful repetitions of this type of experiment, both by LaBerge and by several of his staff members, many scientists still argued that the eye movements might have been accidental. To answer this objection, LaBerge hooked up the polygraph to the muscles in his wrists and went to sleep. In the middle of his first lucid dream, he clenched the left fist of his dream body four times, then the right first once, and finally the left fist twice more. The polygraph revealed that he had spelled out his initials, S.L., in Morse code, an indication of consciousness in a dream that the scientific establishment could no longer dismiss.

LaBerge now trains volunteers to induce lucid dreaming episodes, hoping that he can accumulate a large body of anecdotal evidence to guide further research efforts. His basic advice for lucid dream induction is simple and clear: Record your dreams regularly and look for patterns; underline any repeating element that strikes you as odd; and tell yourself that the next time this element occurs in a dream, you'll consciously recognize it as a sign that you're dreaming.

If you want to experiment more intensively with lucid dreaming, or if you want to increase the frequency of your lucid dreams, you can follow LaBerge's formal training method called MILD (for Mnemonic Induction of Lucid Dreams). Here is a summary of the steps he recommends:

1. Instruct yourself the night before to awaken right after one of your dreams. When you do start waking up from a dream

(which usually happens in the early morning—prime time for lucid dreaming), concentrate on recalling the dream as vividly and completely as possible. Go over it several times until you have memorized it. If you are too tired to keep your mind on your dream, try writing it down, reading, or even meditating for several minutes.

2. As you lie in bed and prepare to resume sleeping, tell yourself, "The next time I'm dreaming, I want to remember to recognize that I'm dreaming." The more calm, sincere determination you can invest in this declaration, the better.

3. Visualize yourself as being back in the dream that you've just had, only this time, have your dream self realize that you are dreaming.

4. Repeat your declaration and visualization (steps two and three) until you fall asleep.

To provide added assistance to novices in lucid dreaming, LaBerge has invented a device he calls the Dream*Light. Shaped like a sleep mask, it contains sensors that detect the rapid eye movements associated with dreaming. Once these sensors are activated, they cause a red light to flash gently off and on, just enough to make the dreamer aware that he or she is dreaming without waking up the dreamer. So far, the Dream*Light is available only through LaBerge's workshops, so that he can integrate its early use-history with supervised training in the MILD technique, but the product may soon be sold on the open market.

Some would-be lucid dreamers practice a less complicated, if more mystical, induction technique adapted from one of the lessons of Don Juan in Carlos Castaneda's book *Journey to Ixtlan*. The objective of this technique is to set yourself up to see your hands in your dream, and to recognize this sight as a sign that you are dreaming (any physical item would do as a target sight, but hands are especially convenient since they are always with you). Several times during the day before you intend to dream lucidly, take a few minutes to relax and focus your attention on your hands. As you study their appearance, tell yourself, "When I see my hands in my dream, I'll know I'm dreaming." Close your eyes, visualize your hands, and repeat your statement of intention. Then open your eyes and look at your hands once more, again repeating your statement of intention.

The key to success in using either the LaBerge or the Castaneda procedure is not intensity but perseverance. You may be lucky and have a long period of lucidity during your very first attempt. Beverly Kedzierski, LaBerge's star oneironaut (the name he gives his volunteers, based on "oneiro," the Greek word for "dream"), is particularly adept at inducing lucid dreams, and she advises against straining or worrying over it. "Simply expect to become lucid and then accept whatever happens," she says. "You really should relax. Do it as something you might enjoy. You will." It may, however take many trials before you experience a fleeting moment of lucid joy in a dream, and usually it takes practice to prolong lucidity to the point where you are actually directing the course of events during your dream.

Whatever the effort, it's well worth it, as I testified from my own dream history in Chapter One. The sensation is definitely one of *living* in another world. In fact, the signal of lucidity in a dream is frequently not the conscious thought "I am dreaming," but a nonverbal physical sensation that is shockingly real and yet strange. Consider this entry from the dream journal of Deborah Jay Hillman, a dream researcher in New York City:

*I became lucid in* [a next-door neighbor's] *back yard in Akron* [Ohio], *near the edge of my own family's yard. A squirrel brushed against my leg. I felt its fur on my bare skin even though I seemed to be wearing long pants. I was* delighted with *the experience of having my full consciousness located in my dream body.*

Commenting on her "squirrel" dream, Hillman says, "In this fleeting episode, the experience of being conscious in my 'dream body' was so novel and extraordinary that I chose to savor it rather than experiment with its possibilities." The possibilities, however, are intoxicating. A retired naval officer in New York City told me about the following dream he had not long after attending a local lucid-dreaming workshop:

*I was wrestling with one of those tiny, tightly wrapped lunch plates on a plane when I heard a softspoken announcement over the p.a. system that the plane would be going to Cuba. I thought surely I must have heard it wrong, that wasn't where we were supposed to go. Then, all of a sudden, a whole row of fierce, ugly-looking terrorists rose up in front of me, holding rifles with sharp bayonets. Their eyes bulged and I knew they were insane. Behind them, I could see into the cockpit. It was empty and I knew they must have gotten rid of the pilot. The plane began shaking, and I was scared out of my wits.*

*But then I realized I was dreaming. I could do what I wanted. I told myself that I'd find an aerosol can of sleeping gas on the seat next to me, and I did. I sprayed it all over the terrorists. Instantly, they dropped to the floor fast asleep. I walked into the cockpit and flew the plane easily and skillfully down to a beach. Then it occurred to me that I was in Cuba, and I'd love to wander across a deserted cove in the moonlight, with the surf pounding along the shoreline. So I left the plane and made night fall. I rounded a nearby hill and there I was in my deserted cove!*

*Walking the beach was just like a favorite memory I have of a night in California forty years ago, only somehow it was more theatrical or super-real. I felt so powerful and just as if I was actually there.*

Aside from being able to master horrible nightmares and indulge pleasurable fantasies, a lucid dreamer possesses an exciting new laboratory for all kinds of practical adventures.

## ■ A lucid dreamer can rehearse difficult behavior.

An assistant vice-president for an East Coast retailer was once nervous about the prospect of giving an important speech in front of four hundred people in the industry. She engineered a lucid dream in which she worked on getting over this nervousness. First she imagined that she was speaking to one or two friends; then, gradually, she "allowed" other people whom she trusted to wander into the room. In time, the room was filled with people—some familiar and some not—who were listening to her with interest and admiration. By then, she felt very comfortable and spoke more eloquently than she ever remembered speaking. Her subsequent waking-life speech went very smoothly and successfully. It was the lucid-dream practice session, she felt, that made the difference.

## ■ A lucid dreamer can work on problems.

A manager at a transportation company in Ohio found himself dreaming lucidly about sitting at his office desk and studying a large map that traced the shipping routes for his company's trucks. Immediately he took advantage of the opportunity. He let his fingers "walk through" the routes to see if he could spot a way to reduce delivery complaints in one of the map's sectors. The information he got from this very literal "dreamwork" was helpful in finally coming to a solution.

## ■ A lucid dreamer can investigate different decision options.

A member of the Brooklyn Dream Community was undecided about which of three presents to give her boyfriend for Christmas:

a lounging robe, a set of oil-painting supplies, or fishing gear. In the course of a lucid dream, she presented all three of these items to her boyfriend and asked him to choose one. When it came time to make her waking-life purchase, her mind was at ease. She went for what her boyfriend had gone for in the dream: the oil-painting supplies.

---

■ **A lucid dreamer can try out creative projects.**

---

A sculptor in Venice, California, once had a lucid dream in which he found himself in a local art gallery. He intentionally imagined his work was on exhibit there. One particular piece—roughly spherical in shape—was a piece he'd been playing with during the past few weeks. In the dream, he made this piece change its shape several times, and each time, he examined how the new shape fit with his other works on exhibit. In the process, he gained some fresh insights about the piece, which he put into action over the next few days.

Talented oneironauts have been performing all these activities and more ever since LaBerge first began popularizing the concept of lucid dreaming almost twenty years ago. Our dreams, LaBerge points out, are often "repetitious melodramas" in which we "confine ourselves by habit to a prison of self-limitation"; lucid dreaming, on the contrary, "presents a way out of this sleep within sleep."

## Waking Dreams

The expression "waking dream" covers a broad range of phenomena. In its purest form, the experience is like an inversion of lucid dreaming. Instead of becoming conscious during a dream, you feel as if you are dreaming while you are technically still awake. Most often, however, a waking dream features a less-pronounced shift in consciousness that leaves you somewhere between waking and dreaming. From this stance, you may be able to witness the dream-like nature of what is commonly called the "real" world, or you may be able to inhabit a dreamscape that exhibits an entirely different kind of reality.

It's possible to fall into a waking dream state involuntarily. It happened a few years ago to Sally Vargo, a Montana homemaker. She was walking through a department store with her daughter when she was suddenly struck with the vision of a fire, as if it were an image projected faintly on a thin scrim between her and her real-world surroundings. Almost at once, the vision became so clear it replaced reality. Vargo saw a house on fire, felt its heat, and heard the screams of children inside the house. Then she caught sight of a woman trying unsuccessfully to get past the flames. Her eyes zeroed in on this figure like a zoom-lens camera: It was her next-door neighbor! Vargo ran screaming for a phone and was intercepted by the store manager. Hearing her babble about her neighbor's house being on fire, he ignored logic and called the fire department himself. When the firefighters arrived at the scene, there was no visible fire. In the basement, however, they discovered a burgeoning electrical fire that would have engulfed the house in flames given a few more minutes.

We don't know what accounts for incidents of consciousness that we call telepathic, clairvoyant, or precognitive, and it is not within the scope of this book to discuss possible explanations. For the purpose of understanding what forms a waking dream can take, however, it's important to be aware that these events *do* happen. The documentary evidence is overwhelming.

Even the eminent historian Arnold Toynbee, in *A Study of History,* confesses to no fewer than six occasions when he was overcome by waking dreams that were appropriate to the particular historical site he happened to be visiting. Clinically known as "retrocognitive" incidents (and further identified by Jung as "psychic localizations"), Toynbee's waking dreams included witnessing the suicide of a proscribed rebel against imperial Rome and listening to an ancient Greek soldier describe his attempt to save a girl from rape.

It's interesting to speculate about how often people have "waking dream" visions that go unconfessed or unrecorded or even unremembered, simply because (a) the dream has no discoverable cross-reference in the real world, (b) it doesn't last long enough to make a strong impression, and/or (c) it is indistinguishable in quality and content from its waking-life surroundings. Perhaps the sensation of *déjà vu* (which we get when we encounter something for the first time, and yet feel that we've encountered it before) is a kind of waking dream: Because something, anything, is causing us to shift momentarily into a dreamlike consciousness, we have a double frame of reference that makes us feel that we have "other knowledge" of the situation.

Strephon Kaplan Williams, founder of the Jungian-Senoi Institute, a dreamwork research and training center in Berkeley, California, and author of *Jungian-Senoi Dreamwork Manual,* finds it therapeutically useful to apply the expression "waking dream" to any intrusion of dream experience into waking life. The intrusion can be merely leakage, such as the inexplicable impulse to purchase an item that, in fact, you dreamed about the night before, or it can be more need-determined. A real-life extramarital affair, for example, may be inspired by a REM-sleep fantasy that is too strong to be contained in one's dream life.

Williams's definition of "waking dream" bids us to see the symbolic, dreamlike quality of our waking-life experiences. Perhaps there is a subconscious meaning behind the accidents that happen to us, or such fateful interventions as robbery, inheritance, rape, love at first sight. Perhaps the synchronicities that link our dream life with our waking life are worth examining more closely: What, for instance, does it say about your world if you dream of an Japanese immigrant during the night and unwittingly wind up watching a TV show about a Japanese immigrant during the day?

Certainly analyzing our existence from these atypical perspectives can alert us to forces, motivations, and patterns that might otherwise go unrecognized.

More commonly, dreamworkers characterize a waking dream as a state of mind that the subject *voluntarily* invokes. The ultimate vision-seeking project of this type is the shamanic journey. Shamans are men and women who develop the ability, through training and self-discipline, to enter planes of "nonordinary" reality by way of their imagination. The status of "shaman" (whether or not it is so named) and the shamanic journey itself are core elements of virtually every spiritual tradition in human history, and the "nonordinary" realities to which the shamans journey are generally worlds that reflect a psychological as well as a cosmological hierarchy.

Stanley Krippner, director for Consciousness Studies at Saybrook Institute in San Francisco and an expert on shamanism, provides an enlightening summary of the conceptual background that informs most shamanic journeys—a background that will sound familiar to any reader of *Genesis:*

> *In the myths of many primitive cultures, there are accounts of three cosmic zones—earth, heaven, and the underworld—and the ease by which people could* [traverse] *them. For example, there* [were] *no rigid divisions between wakefulness and dreams; people could create from their dreams actions in the waking world.... After the "fall" of humankind, due to some type of sin, arrogance, or violation of sacred rules, the bridge collapsed; travel between the zones became the sole privilege of deities, spirits, and shamans. (from Stanley Krippner, "Shamanism and Dreams,"* Dream Network Bulletin, *March–April 1984, p. 14)*

Once an individual receives the call to be a shaman (typically in a dream), he or she learns through virtue, humility, and ritual to reactivate the "traveling" powers that lie dormant and unrealized in the minds of all human beings. As preparation for a journey, a shaman may sing, dance, chant, or meditate to free his or her mind from the concerns and rhythms of ordinary life. The journey itself is typically driven by a constant, monotonous drumbeat that casts the shaman into an altered state of consciousness resembling the hypnagogic moment that precedes sleep. Powered by an imaginative force similar to visualization, the shaman explores a "nonordinary" reality whose features and creatures bear an inherently symbolic relationship to aspects of ordinary reality.

Today, in addition to the classic tribal shamanism that is still practiced in many parts of the world (including Indian reservations in the United States), there is a "neoshamanic" movement, consisting of individuals from all walks of life and all religious backgrounds who pursue shamanic studies and incorporate shamanic rituals into their own personal or group spiritual quests. Many of these individuals are also dreamworkers: It's a natural and logical connection.

Tom Cowan, founder of the Brooklyn Dream Community, belongs to a neoshamanic group in New York City that was trained by Michael Harner, an anthropologist who has studied shamanism extensively in the field and who now conducts workshops across the United States and the Soviet Union through the auspices of the Center for Shamanic Studies in Norwalk, Connecticut. Cowan believes that shamanic work and dreamwork complement each other in a singularly rewarding way. Speaking of what he has learned through journeying with his neoshamanic group, he remarks:

> By entering that specialized state of consciousness on a regular basis and with the support of others, we enrich both our waking and dreaming lives, for often what we learn and experience in the Other Worlds will recur in our dreams at night, and often images and situations from a journey will manifest themselves in an ordinary state of consciousness at odd moments during our average day.
>
> In our dreams at night, we often enter that realm of archetypes, gods, goddesses, and spirits that appear to us in the various guises of our dream imagery. In our dreamwork, we learn how to see through and into those images to recognize the "god or spirit within." In a similar fashion, shamans, both ancient and modern, cultivate those presences, enlist their power on terms of friendship and stewardship, and harness that power in

*whatever form of insight, knowledge, or understanding is available to enrich their own lives and the lives of the group.*

A more accessible, if less dramatic, type of voluntary waking dream can be obtained through meditation or visualization (which, briefly defined, is the deliberate formation of mental images to express thoughts and feelings). No matter how loosely you structure these activities, they have the capacity to alter your normal state of consciousness, so that you are better equipped to generate and process the "nonordinary" type of material that is associated with your dream life.

Here are some of the ways you can use meditation and visualization to experience a waking dream:

- Replay a recent dream in your mind, allowing the images to flow as spontaneously and unchecked as they did when you originally had the dream. You may recall details in the dream that your conscious mind missed.

- Isolate major images in a recent dream and focus on them, one at a time, in separate meditation or visualization exercises. This activity can unlock the symbolic significance as well as the creative potential of the images.

- Reenter a recent dream and explore different points of view or different options. In this manner, you may not only get a fresh slant on the subject matter of that specific dream, but also condition your dreaming mind to handle the same or similar subject matter in different ways.

- Reenter a recent dream and continue it beyond the point at which it originally stopped. This exercise offers a wealth of new insights into the dream itself and into the way your mind works.

- Pick a subject (such as a meaningful image, a relationship, a goal in your life, a problem that you want to solve) and allow your mind to weave a story about it. Like a dream story, it doesn't need to have a logical plot or an ending, just a developing stream of images. This activity will add to your knowledge about the subject you've chosen, and it will educate you about the way in which dreams in general take shape.

■ Have someone you trust and respect guide you through a visualization. There are many possible routes your guide can take, including:
  ■ following one of the many published examples of visualizations
  ■ spinning a creative story in which you are the central figure
  ■ recounting one of your dreams or an episode from your waking life
  ■ recounting one of his or her dreams or an episode from his or her waking life, with you as the central character

The advantage of a guided meditation or visualization is that you can be even more relaxed and receptive to the drift of your thoughts, which will give your imagination more flexibility. If you try out either of the last two possibilities, you set the stage for a much deeper communion between you and your guide regarding dream life and waking life.

## Dream Buddies

"We are as alone as in our dreams." Jean-Paul Sartre's existential lament about life applies with added poignance to people yearning to share their interest in dreams with others. Dreams do lend themselves admirably to solitary dreamwork, but the self-study approach can easily become claustrophobic. You bury your nose in your dream journal and it's as if you were trapped in a house of mirrors. Not only do you grow frustrated seeing the same old face in each of your dreams, you also wind up retracing your steps again and again, unable to break out of your usual routines of dream interpretation and analysis.

For many people, the solution to the house-of-mirrors syndrome is to share dreams and dreamwork activities regularly with someone else. The two of you can trade insights about specific images and patterns in each other's dreams, monitor similarities and contrasts that occur over time in each other's dreams, and use each other's dreams as springboards to creative thinking. The format of your exchange can be as open-ended or as structured as the two of you want to make it, depending upon the nature of your relationship and your relative dreamwork interests and skills.

You may want to begin by "adopting" each other's dreams. It's such a simple and rewarding dream-buddy endeavor that you may decide to make it a standard practice in your relationship. In a typical dream-adoption session, you take turns pretending your dream buddy's dream happened to you. You articulate how *you* would feel about such a dream and what it might mean in the context of *your* life. This helps the original dreamer of the dream to step aside from his or her waking-life frame of reference and see the dream in an entirely different light. It also enables you to comment on possible meanings of the dream without directly (and presumptuously) interpreting what the dream means in terms of your buddy's life.

One of the most important rules in dreamwork is that the dreamer is the sole authority on the meaning of his or her own dream. Others can certainly make contributions toward a better understanding of the dream, but they should not try to usurp the role of interpreter. That role can only properly be filled by the dreamer, who produced and witnessed the dream on his or her own.

The dream-adoption strategy is one way to make sure you don't step over the fine line that separates discussion from interpretation when you're working on someone else's dream. If you recast a buddy's dream as your own dream, then you become the dreamer, and you're free to talk about it and interpret it as you will. As your buddy listens, he or she can draw any meaningful connections between what you say and what he or she feels about the dream.

Another way for you and your dream buddy to make sure that you work on each other's dreams constructively, rather than imposing interpretations on each other, is to engage in a dialogue similar to that which typically occurs between a professional therapist and a dreamer. In this dialogue, the nondreamer steadfastly maintains the role of questioner, prompting the dreamer to recreate the dream as completely and as vividly as possible, to express his or her feelings during and after the dream, to identify key images and patterns, and to explain the relevance of any dream material to his or her waking life. Only after the dreamer feels he or she has reached a good understanding of the meaning of the dream should the questioner volunteer any commentary.

In describing this kind of interview approach in her book *Living Your Dreams,* Gayle Delaney stresses the value of getting the dreamer (or, as she says, the "producer") to *define* images that appear in his or her dream. For example, if you're the questioner and the dream is about crossing a stream and finding a birdcage in a bush, you would make a point of asking the dreamer: "What's a stream?" "What's a birdcage?" "What's a bush?" This forces the dreamer to articulate his or her uniquely personal understanding of what these images are, which can make their symbolic importance more apparent. It's something a dreamer is not likely to do except in the context of a question-and-answer dialogue with someone else. Delaney advises:

> *You may find the producer more willing to answer your* [definition] *questions if you first ask him to pretend that you come from another planet. This way, when you ask him, "Who is Bob Hope?" he won't simply answer, "You know who Bob Hope is!" and miss the opportunity of discovering his associations to the man. So often what a dreamer assumes to be general knowledge or fact about a given figure or event is really a very personal web of attitudes, beliefs, and associations. Ask the producer to be as patient with you as you will be with him. (from* Gayle Delaney, Living Your Dreams, New York: Harper & Row, *1981, p. 52)*

The same truth applies to even the most commonplace objects. Subconsciously, we invest them with all sorts of connotations that never get formally expressed; therefore, we never consciously realize them unless we're challenged to do so. We assume, for example, that a rose is a rose to us and everyone else, when in fact (Gertrude Stein notwithstanding) a rose means something very different to each of us. One of the principal benefits of working on dreams with a buddy is that we arrive at a better understanding of our own dream symbology by being forced to examine it from our buddy's perspective, as well as by comparing it to our buddy's personal dream symbology.

If your dream buddy is a lover, or a spouse, or a resident family member—someone who shares your living and dreaming space—the time spent together on dreamwork can be especially meaningful. In addition to giving you an opportunity to know each other better through your dreams, it can also function as an ideal context for discussing other personal matters. Some of these personal matters may have a direct bearing on the dream material, while others may relate to the feelings, images, or issues that arise in the course of talking about a dream. In either case, you have established a nonjudgmental forum with your dream-buddy relationship that will make discussion of even the most sensitive topics much easier and much more productive.

Often you will find that you and your lover, spouse, or family member have similar dreams on the same night, or a similar repertoire of dreams over an extended period. In March of 1985, Dr. Edward Bruce Taub-Bynum, a family therapist, submitted a call for family dreams of this nature to readers of the *Dream Network Bulletin* and offered this personal experience as an example:

> . . . *after a sleep-filled night in December, my wife and I mentioned our dreams to each other as is our custom. I had dreamed a strange dream in which a "grandmother type" was trying to reach or catch me. She triggered "mixed feelings" in me as to whether she was trying to protect me or somehow "get me." Also in the dream the grandmother attempted to steal*

*or cut off a pickle I had! Having a somewhat Freudian lens, I made note of the sexual aspect of this. I later woke with a slightly eerie feeling.*

*On the same night my wife dreamed my grandmother had a necklace with a moon-shaped crescent locket which fell partly from her neck and turned into a knife or sharp edge. My wife then wondered in the dream whether the grandmother was gay.*

Apart from what each dream—or both dreams—symbolized, Taub-Bynum was most struck by the major images they had in common: the grandmother who was associated with abnormal sex and the act of cutting. It provided further evidence of a dream-related phenomenon he had been observing for years. As he explains:

*While on a post-doctoral fellowship, I had the opportunity to study the dreams of families in therapy. To my surprise, we discovered that recurrent patterns of interaction and behavior are reflected in the dreams of each family member. This was especially true when the family was going through a crisis or some intense situation.*

*What we discovered was a field of shared images, ideas, and feelings in each individual within the family. This shared family emotional field, which we call the family unconscious, is a shifting, interconnected field of energy. . . . A certain kind of hologram appears in which each part can reflect all the other parts in slightly different ways.*

Regardless of how intimate you are with your dream buddy during your waking life, a similar effect can happen over time. You will not only "borrow" images, motifs, and plots from each other's dreams, you will also literally dream of each other from time to time. The result in any case is a richer, more variegated dream life, even if you only tell each other your dreams and leave it at that.

## Dream Groups

In a dream-buddy relationship, you quickly learn that two heads are much better than one when it comes to probing the elusive and multidimensional meanings of a dream. How much better, then, are three heads, four heads, five heads, or more. Like any form of theater, dreams revolve around the interplay between a human being and the public domain, so it seems fitting that one of the best settings for dreamwork, if not *the* best, is within a group of sympathetic dreamers.

As soon as you begin exposing your individual dreams to the collective imagination, you start gaining new appreciation and respect for them. Even a dream of yours that you initially think is silly, embarrassing, or worthless invariably turns out to be a fresh glimpse into the dreaming experience for each of the other group members, and seeing it through all these different sets of eyes, you become much more sensitive to the special insights it has to offer.

Soon, you will find that you remember your dreams more clearly and dream more purposefully, because you have a new responsibility in dreaming: You've broken away from solitary confinement and entered a community. It's a step that serves you as well as humankind. In the words of Dr. Montague Ullman, "In so-called civilized societies, there exists a need for people to share intimate parts of themselves in a safe, social context. In dream groups, people learn that sharing and self-disclosure are the first steps toward communion."

A psychiatrist and psychoanalyst who has studied dreams in and out of the laboratory for over thirty years, Ullman has taken a leading role in promoting and training nonprofessional dream groups in both the United States and Scandinavia, where he spends four months a year. The method he designed for working on a dream within a group is a highly popular one for two important reasons: First, it gives everyone a flexible and attractive framework for talking about the dream, and an equal chance to participate, which results in a lot of creative input for the dreamer (Ullman calls this aspect of the process "the discovery factor"); and second, it ensures that the dreamer retains the right to accept or reject any comments that are offered and to discuss the dream as he or she chooses (Ullman calls this aspect of the process "the safety factor").

Ullman outlines the complete process in two different books—
*Working With Dreams* (coauthored with Nan Zimmerman; New York:
J.P. Tarcher, Inc., 1979) and *The Variety of Dream Experience* (edited in
conjunction with Claire Zimmer, M.S.; New York: Continuum,
1987). Here is a brief summary of the basic stages in the process:

1. The dreamer recites a dream in the present tense, either from
   memory or from a written record. The latter is generally preferable since it provides a fixed source of reference for later discussion of the dream.

   In some groups, the members may choose to write down the
   dream—word for word—as the dreamer recites it, so that
   they can "buy into" the dream more fully, as well as have their
   own reference copies. In other groups, the members may
   choose to close their eyes and visualize the dream as it is being
   told, so that they can "dream" the dream for themselves.

   In any event, the group members silently listen until the
   dreamer is finished. Then they may ask brief questions to clarify
   images and events in the dream that they don't understand.

2. The group members make the dream their own, *i.e.*, each person pretends that the dream is one he or she has had and speaks
   of it accordingly. Meanwhile, the dreamer remains silent and
   unaddressed and "eavesdrops" on the conversation.

   There are two parts to the conversation. First, individual
   group members share (spontaneously, as the spirit moves them)
   the *feelings* that their dream contains and evokes (*e.g.*, "In my
   dream, I feel angry when the fat man slaps me" or "The colors
   in my dream excite me"). Second, individual group members
   talk about metaphors, symbols, and patterns that they see in
   their dream (*e.g.*, "I notice in my dream that there are a number
   of circular images, as if I were going round and round and not
   getting anywhere" or "In my dream, I think the tall stranger
   represents my father, who was away from home a great deal").

3.  When the discussion has run its course, the dream is returned to the dreamer. If the dreamer wishes to comment on the dream and/or the group discussion, then all group members remain silent and the dreamer responds as he or she wishes.

    Often, the dreamer reiterates statements made by group members that did or did not "strike home," but this type of response is not necessary. If the dreamer wants, he or she can talk about the waking-life context of the dream and then invite open-ended questions, at which point a dialogue can take place between the dreamer and the rest of the group. These questions should be aimed not at interpreting the dream for the dreamer, but at eliciting more information that might have a bearing on the dream's meaning, so that the dreamer can better determine the meaning of the dream.

4.  As a way of closing the group's work on the dream, one of the group members (generally the group leader for that particular meeting) may want to make what Ullman refers to as an "orchestrating projection." This effort consists of organizing what the dreamer has shared into an image-by-image explanation of what the dream appears to be communicating. In creating this summary interpretation of the dream, it is important to include only information and ideas that the dreamer has acknowledged as relevant. In listening to this summary interpretation of the dream, it is important to bear in mind that what is being said constitutes only a projection of what the dream may mean— not a definitive translation.

5.  Between this meeting and the next one, the dreamer reviews the dream and the dream discussion. If any additional thoughts or insights emerge during this time, the dreamer may want to share them with the group.

While the Ullman method has many advantages for both novice and experienced dreamworkers, it is difficult to work on more than one dream per hour. There are many other, less time-consuming and less formal dreamwork techniques suitable for groups of five to eight (which is a good size—large enough for variety and yet small enough for lots of individual participation). You could try Gayle Delaney's "interview" method (as mentioned earlier in this chapter and as detailed in her book *Living Your Dreams*), or reentering dreams through visualization, or some form of "gestalt" dreamwork, in which group members dramatically recreate a dream (see Ann Faraday's *The Dream Game*, New York: Harper & Row, 1973, and *Dream Power*, New York: Harper & Row, 1974, for ideas). You could adopt a "workshop" approach, in which each meeting explores a different way of working with dreams (for example, drawing your dreams, using the tarot to "decode" your dreams, or applying the teachings of a particular dream scholar to your dreams). Two books that offer a wealth of group dreamwork strategies are Jeremy Taylor's *Dream Work* (New York: Paulist Press, 1983) and Jill Morris's *The Dream Workbook* (Boston: Little, Brown, 1985).

As I mentioned in Chapter One, "Dreams and Dreamwork," existing dream groups frequently recruit new members through classified ads, especially in campus or free press periodicals. Some of these groups are, in fact, large, open-ended networks that can put you in touch with smaller groups. The bible of dream networking, *Dream Network Bulletin*, carries announcements of dream groups from all over the country (editor, Linda Magallon; mailing address, 1083 Harvest Meadow Court, San Jose, California 94947).

If you wish to start your own dream group, veteran dream-networker Tom Cowan offers these suggestions:

■ Don't try to organize a dream group alone. Get a friend with an interest in dreams to help you. Everyone starting up a new venture can use a partner for moral support and for generating new ideas.

■ Form a clear picture of the kind of dream group members you'd like to have. You may want to assemble a group of people with similar backgrounds and interests (for example, the same age, sex, marital status, occupation, avocation, or hobby). On Long Island, there is a dream group of mothers with small children. In Manhattan, there's a dream group of writers. On scores of campuses, there are dream groups of students majoring in the same subject or living in the same residence. A homogeneous dream group has obvious advantages because you dream and speak from a pool of shared experiences. On the other hand, a group of people having diverse ages, interests, and backgrounds can illuminate a dream from many excitingly different perspectives.

■ Announce your intention to form a dream club in as many sympathetic places as are available to you. You might try New Age bookstores, health food shops, and community service bulletin boards (*e.g.*, at local Y's, college campuses, senior citizen centers, and neighborhood meeting places). Run free ads in neighborhood newspapers and community announcement spots on local radio stations. Call the psychology department of a local college and ask to speak to some professor with an interest in dreams who might be willing to mention your dream group to classes. In your announcements, have people phone you or your friend, so that you can do some initial screening and work out a time for the first meeting that suits the majority of people.

■ Let the first meeting be an open house at which you introduce yourselves, get to know one another, and share your interests in dreams. Each person should have an opportunity to address everyone present and explain why he or she likes dreams, and what types of dreamwork he or she usually performs.

■ Before the first meeting is over, decide the basic mechanics of how the dream group will operate: how often you will meet and what you will try to accomplish in the meetings. If you have a large response to your announcements, say ten or more people, you may want to form two separate groups. Each member of a group should be able to commit him- or herself to *all* of the projected meetings, so that the group can better develop the trust, understanding, and appreciation for one another that are essential for effective group dreamwork.

- Once you get started, each group meeting will require someone to act as facilitator. You can either rotate this role each meeting or choose one person to handle it regularly. In any event, the leader is not to be considered "the expert" or "the judge." In dream groups, all members are equal and all dreams are equal. The facilitator's role is simply to begin the dreamwork process, keep it going, and bring it to a smooth conclusion.

- Don't be discouraged if only three or four people respond to your call for dreamers. Some dreamers, you know, are still asleep! If you find no one else interested at the time, you've still got your partner, who can become a dream buddy. In time, as the two of you talk about your dream explorations with relatives, friends, neighbors, and coworkers, you'll find others will want to join you. "Dream on," Cowan advises, "and remember that we do not dream for ourselves alone."

## A World of Dreamers

Cowan's plea—"Dream on, and remember that we do not dream for ourselves alone"—recalls us to the central point of this book. Our dreams constitute a second life, one that is inextricably linked with our waking life as well as with the dream lives and waking lives of others who share our world. Potentially, dreams can connect all human beings, and for that reason alone, they are worth our individual and collective time, attention, and care.

In 1954, Kilton Stewart, an anthropologist, claimed to have discovered a dream-driven utopia in the depths of Malaysia's Cameron Highlands. According to his report, the Temiar Senoi, a tribe of about ten thousand people, structured their lives around dream sharing; and it was his belief that this practice accounted for the virtual absence in their society of any serious crime or conflict as well as the low incidence of mental and physical disease.

Every morning, Stewart said, Senoi family members shared dreams and explored ways to respond positively to what their dreams seemed to be saying. For example, if a child were to dream that a friend attacked him, his father might advise him to be especially nice to that person and to resolve any areas of disagreement between them. Every evening, important dreams would be discussed in community councils, and insights derived from discussing these dreams would be woven into the fabric of daily Senoi life.

Since Stewart's report, dream enthusiasts (like Ann Faraday) and anthropologists (like Robert Knox Dentan) have revisited the Senoi tribes and have been disappointed to find very few traces of institutionalized dreamwork. Was Stewart lying? Did Senoi translators mislead him? Or had the Senoi culture, already weakening from outside infiltration in Stewart's time, deteriorated to the point that dreams were no longer so highly valued?

As is often the case with anthropological research (consider, for example, the controversial career of Margaret Mead) and as is almost always the case with dreams, what's real and what's false become virtually meaningless issues. What matters is the image that has already made its indelible impression. The idea that the Senoi people lived and therefore thrived by their dreams is a powerful and inspiring force.

I mention the Senoi report at the close of this book because it represents what to me is the ideal dreamwork situation—a whole society of people who not only live their waking lives together but also share one another's dreams. I can't help but believe it would be a good thing if every society on earth were to follow this example on a neighborhood-by-neighborhood basis. With such a depth of communion among people and such a wealth of different life possibilities brought to light, it's difficult to imagine that we wouldn't live in a more peaceful, more productive, and more enjoyable world. As Jack Kerouac once said: "All human beings are also dream beings. Dreaming ties all mankind together."